VINTAGE RACING!! START TO FINISH

A Complete Guide to the Exciting World of Vintage Racing

"**VINTAGE RACING!! START TO FINISH** is must reading for anyone involved in the sport of vintage racing."—AUGIE PABST

"The sport of vintage racing is a great opportunity to fulfill a lifetime dream... a fun sport that recreates auto racing history. What vintage racing is all about is a love affair with the automobile... it doesn't matter how fast it runs or where it finishes in the race - it's there to see, enjoy and drive. **VINTAGE RACING!! START TO FINISH** is an enjoyable, worthwhile book... should be read by all."—RODGER WARD

"In racing, the Start/Finish lines are usually the same. Vintage racing is thus being sublimely true to its nature in bringing the old cars back for another lap in the limelight. The old sounds, the old smells, the old sense of fun for the fun of it. Recycled joy. Some of the old people, too. But the best thing is that vintage racing is more that a mere rerun of the old days, it's a rebirth of the *spirit* of those times, too. New people respond to it just as we did when these cars were factory-fresh — some because they missed it on the first lap, some because through some oversight they didn't exist then. I'm delighted that *Jim McCarthy* has produced an accessible and thorough guide in **VINTAGE RACING!! START TO FINISH** for all those drawn to the sport from whatever time for whatever reason. Come on in, get your sump wet. Are we having fun or what?!"—DENISE MCCLUGGAGE-Senior Contributing Editor, <u>AUTOWEEK</u> and current participant in vintage racing.

VINTAGE RACING!! START TO FINISH

A Complete Guide to the
Exciting World of Vintage Racing

by

Jim McCarthy

Foreword by
Dewey Dellinger

Illustrations by
James Wyanski

Published by
RPM Enterprises LTD
Motorsport International Publishing Company
(MIPCO)

rpm enterprises ltd.

For any additional information contact:
Jim McCarthy
Rt. 3, Box 45
Sparta, WI 54656

First Edition 1990

2   3   4   5   6   7   8   9   10

Library of Congress Catalog Card Number 90-060140

McCarthy, Jim
Vintage Racing!! Start to Finish

ISBN   0-9625532-0-4

TABLE OF CONTENTS

PREFACE

by John Fitch

Any remarks of mine have to be suspect in that I personally <u>am</u> VINTAGE, and to me these vintage cars are the real cars. They're large and small, with performance often intriguingly inverse to their size. They are distinctive with never a question of their identity in this day of lookalikes. They have <u>CHARACTER</u>.

Those who forget the past are destined to repeat it. We didn't really forget the racing of the past, it was just out of mind for awhile, which may be why racing is being repeated with such style and elegance. The revival is obviously in good hands and it may be because these competent managers are closer of an age with the instrument of their sport, the cars themselves. These more mature officials have honed their talents for administration, logistics and organization in their professional fields and apply them with the skills of the pros that they are.

One of the best events, for example is the Pittsburgh Vintage Gran Prix held in the stunning Schenley Park in the city center. The city and many of its departments, industry, business interests and the community at large, to the tune of 900 volunteers are totally involved in this event and with the several charities it supports.

The spirit and the objectives of the vintage movement are unquestionably laudable in every sense. But there's a catch and it is that racers will be racers unless they understand and accept the *spirit* of vintage racing. Those elements of the psyche that make a race driver are not easily inhibited by an edict, notwithstanding that it is based on a valid premise. To be candid,

I have observed the race driver, not necessarily a cerebral-directed creature, but that he or she possesses certain qualities: a spatial orientation, a keen sense of balance and a grasp of inertia, the momentum and the dynamics that come into play in the passage of a race car over a given surface.

In a racing circumstance, an awareness of these factors enters a racing driver's mind (his computer) and the command to 'go for it' flashes. The result is, he goes for it, as much a spectator to his own actions as an uninvolved bystander. Going for it with zeal is not the result of any cerebral process or prompting, but a purely instinctive act triggered by his total race driver makeup as it reads the circumstances. That is the *derigueur* in normal racing, but not in the *vintage* concept. Behavior modification is in order and I'm happy to say I know first hand it can be done.

In his day, Stirling Moss intended to win every race he entered. By consummate skill, by tactics, by strategy, by opportunism (in the play by ear, not the trickster sense)—by any legitimate means he intended to win and he very often did. Stirling, the charger personified has come to terms with vintage racing and with himself as they interface. He no longer "tigers", possessed to win but plays his part at a docile 7/10ths, in a new role for him (perhaps 4/10ths on his exalted scale would be sufficient). Having raced for some years both with and against Stirling and against him more recently in vintage events, I know whereof I speak. If Stirling Moss can be converted to the vintage attitude, we all can. And with the outstanding management in charge, vintage will continue its spectacular success. We will all be the winners for it.

For anyone interested in participating at any level, this book uniquely articulates the vintage philosophy and provides the information needed to know what it's all about and how to do it right. It is well written and entertaining as well as informative. I recommend it without reservation.

John Fitch
January, 1990

John Fitch is a former world class race car driver for Mercedes, Jaguar and Porsche, a current participant in vintage racing and author of the book Adventure on Wheels—*an autobiography of his illustrious racing career from the 50's and 60's.*

John Fitch, behind the wheel of a C-Type Jaguar before the start of the 1952 'Seneca Cup' at Watkins Glen, New York.

ACKNOWLEDGMENTS

The author would like to give thanks to Dewey Dellinger for his encouragement and support and to Henry Adamson of the Vintage Sports Car Drivers Association for his contribution to Chapter I (A Short History...). Also, to the many vintage racing related businesses who helped support the production of this book. To Dick LeBlanc for his kind response and artistic talents and to Darleen Loewenstein for taking the time to help edit. To my intelligent 12 year old son, Michael, the family 'computer whiz' for his word processing knowledge and skills. Lastly, to my wife for her patience, understanding, encouragement and editing skills.

DEDICATION

...to the sport of vintage racing and the people who make it happen...may future generations experience the enjoyment, excitement, history, beauty and function of classic and historical automobiles through the medium we call VINTAGE RACING.

FOREWORD

The sport of racing vintage sports cars, which began long ago in Europe and other areas, traces its roots in North America to the forming of the Vintage Sports Car Club of America in 1959. Since that time the number of other clubs and organizations which have formed to provide a place for vintage auto enthusiasts to play has increased dramatically, as have the number of participants, both behind the wheel and looking on.

This growth, which has escalated most rapidly in the last five years, is both good and bad for the sport.

The good part of the equation comes from the fact that we now have over 100 vintage racing events a year in North America with at least one event every month. We also have more people enjoying the sport, either by driving cars or participating as crew, workers or spectators. The number of cars currently turned out for events by their owners has multiplied as well so that on any given weekend one is likely to find full grids of production cars, sports racers, many different formulas, etc., making for quite a show.

The bad portion is that, as in any type of progress some innocence is lost and what started out as a few people getting together to enjoy their cars at speed has evolved for the most part into something rather different. Today, one finds some cars being prepared more for speed than for era authenticity, with driving attitudes to match. This variance on a good idea has put a strain on the race organizers and the technical inspectors who try to govern what and who goes on the track at a vintage race weekend. Fortunately, the organizers have recognized this problem and are presently dealing with it to ensure the longevity of the sport in the vein in which it was originally conceived.

Which brings us to the primary purpose of this book, VIN-TAGE RACING!! START TO FINISH. Even though this is somewhat of a "how to" book, the seasoned vintage racer should also read and cultivate the story between its pages, paying close attention to what constitutes the true spirit of vintage racing. Maintaining a balance of cars properly prepared and drivers with the right attitude are fundamental to preserving the sport that exists today. Vintage racing is not about racing old cars. It is much more, and what it is needs to be well understood by all who participate within its guidelines. Perhaps the mission statement of the Vintage Motorsports Council, the coordinating body for many North America's vintage sports car racing organizations says it best:

"The primary objective of the sport of Vintage and Historical automobile racing is to promote the preservation of these cars in a racing format which emphasizes driver safety and etiquette.

The sport is intended to provide a format for friendly wheel-to-wheel competition with vehicles faithfully prepared to their era.

All racing is dangerous and only the proper attitude of the driver and the careful preparation of the cars will diminish the danger and will enhance our appreciation of this sport."

The era to which this message relates is one that is commonly referred to as "gentleman's racing". Today, this means that winning at all costs is forbidden.

The same is true of any car owner who prepares a racer beyond the design capabilities of the era in which the car participated. This does not mean that cars should not have new brake linings, structurally sound roll bars or master electrical cut-off switches. These items can help preserve the life of the car and its driver in case of an incident.

Vintage racing is a family and friends fun-oriented sport involving classic sports cars in a social racing setting.

As you can see, what this all boils down to is <u>attitude</u>, both for those preparing the car for competition in the garage and for the person sitting behind the wheel of the racer on the track.

This book should give you all you need to know about getting started in the sport of vintage and historic sports car racing. Read it well and you will know the <u>spirit</u>, too. Somewhere in these many pages you will realize that this is the sport for you, or not. To the veteran vintage racer, in the process of reading this book, take the time to evaluate your reasons for participating in vintage racing. Are they in line with the *spirit* of the sport?

If you feel that you have the temperament that would be thrilled with safely driving a properly prepared racing car from the romantic days gone-by at speed with others of its era, then welcome to the sport!

DEWEY DELLINGER
FOUNDER
VICTORY LANE MAGAZINE
PRESIDENT
Vintage Motorsports Council

INTRODUCTION

SO YOU WANT TO GO VINTAGE RACING...?

The popularity of vintage racing has grown tremendously over the past few years with nearly 100 vintage racing events taking place in 1989. At Road Atlanta, Laguna Seca and other major race tracks across the nation hardly a weekend passes without enthusiasts hearing and seeing the great marques of the past roaring down the front straightaways - titillating the senses and invoking exciting memories of yesteryear. Classic racing cars of the past have risen from the dust and have been brought back to life in living color.

Many famous people who helped create, design, fabricate, maintain, and *race* these moving works of art have also returned to share in the excitement and nostalgia. The racing greats of the past are at it again as they drive the same cars that brought them victory and fame in the 50's, 60's and 70's. The unique experience of watching the Master, Stirling Moss, maneuver the victorious 1960 Mille Miglia Tipo 61 "Birdcage" Maserati through Laguna Seca's famous corkscrew causes the blood to rush and spirit to rise. Seeing Jim Hall's awesome V-8 powered Chapparal take the same racing lines as it did over 20 years ago on its way to a resounding and stunning victory at the 1965 Twelve Hours of Sebring invokes memories when the United States was king of the hill in international sports car racing. In addition, the designers/managers are involved with the resurgence of these classic racing machines. In recent years, the late John Wyer was seen in attendance at Road Atlanta during the Sportscar Vintage Racing Association (SVRA) celebration of Aston Martin's 1959 World Sports Car Championship. The experience of walking through the paddock with this giant of the past, as he explains his commitment and involvement with Aston Martin, elicits a certain respect and awe for a man who was a living testament to the glory days of sports car racing. In 1989, the Vintage Sports Car Drivers Association (VSCDA) hosted the 30th Anniversary of Formula Junior at Elkhart Lake's Road America in Wisconsin. Participating in the festivities, and acting as Honorary Grand Marshall was Count Giovanni (Johnny) Lurani from Italy. The famous Count Lurani played an integral part in the birth and growth of Formula Junior racing in the late 50's. This exciting class of racing was the training ground for many championship drivers of the past and present. Joining the Count were Frank Nichols, father of Elva, and Peter Arundell, the winningest driver during the Formula Junior period. Also, during 1989 at Watkins Glen, the SVRA hosted the 25th anniversary celebration of Ford's GT-40. Over 35 famous "40's" from around the world took part in the reunion, including the actual cars that won at Le Mans in the middle 60's that ended Ferrari's domination of the Sarthe Circuit. There seems to be no end to the special events that are occuring in vintage racing. In 1990, 12 famous vintage racing Austin-Healey's from Europe will compete in the North American Healey Challenge at several race tracks, including Mid-Ohio, Elkhart Lake, Watkins Glen, Lime Rock and others.

The above represents a very small part of what is happening in vintage racing today. The statistics prove that over the past few years there has been a proliferation of vintage racing organizations, events and participants. Coupled with this increase is a tremendous growth in spectator interest and support. Also involved is a continual explosion of information that is constantly evolving and changing. If you have been a follower or interested spectator and want to experience the movement - what is the next logical step? How does one go about preparing for the exciting world of vintage racing? What follows is a sequential account to assist the aspiring vintage racer in acquiring rookie status and a solid foundation in vintage racing. In addition, the veteran racer can use this book as a quick reference guide on vintage racing in general. It will assist you in determining whether you and your vintage racer are eligible for racing in other organizations and events. Also, the book contains invaluable information on vintage racing related services, parts and supplies.

To all currently involved with the sport of vintage racing and to those enthusiasts who want to participate in the sport with hopes of developing some staying power - adjust your seat belts and set those mirrors...the goal is *fun* and *finishing*.

THUMBS UP AND HAVE A GREAT RACE!!!
Jim McCarthy

Count Johnny Lurani (2nd from left), father of Formula Junior, acting as Honorary Grand Marshall during the VSCDA's 1989 Elkhart Lake Vintage Fall Festival, celebrating 30 years of Formula Junior.

JAMES WYANSKI © '89

CHAPTER I

PRE-RACE WARM-UP...A SHORT HISTORY & CURRENT STATUS

"vintage racing is the fastest growing motorsport in terms of participants and spectators"

The first known organization devoted to racing 'old cars' was founded in England in 1934. The Vintage Sports Car Club (VSCC) was touted as a club for the not-so-rich and allowed racing for sport cars of at least 5 years of age, and/or defunct of manufacture. When operations ceased in 1939, the VSCC was one of the most active motorcar organizations in Britain.

At about the same time the VSCC was formed, the New England States saw the birth of an organization which was, in effect, very similar to the VSCC. This was the Automobile Racing Club of America (ARCA) founded by brothers Sam and Miles Collier. Dedicated to a "European" style of racing, the earliest events were on the drives of the Colliers' estate in Pocantico Hills. By the late 30's some of the races were being held on the streets of slightly seedy up-country resorts— shades of Watkins Glen and Elkhart Lake to come. When operations ceased at the end of 1940, the ARCA fields were seeing a large number of 'modern' cars with no venue for racing old cars.

After WWII, ARCA reformed and changed its name to the Sports Car Club of America (SCCA). The earliest SCCA events at Watkins Glen and Bridgehampton looked a great deal like those run by ARCA in the late 30's, but pre-war sport cars and specials soon gave way to Jaguar, MG, Healey and Porsche.

In 1958, Ralph Loucks and Vale Faro drove Ralph's Locomobile roadster out to Long Island for the 50th Anniversary of George Robertson's winning the Vanderbilt Cup in a Locomobile. They encountered the crew, led by Edgar Roy, who were trying to bring about the Vintage Sports Car Club of America (VSCCA). Faro and Loucks had the gospel preached to them and carried it back to the Midwest and helped form the Inland Region of the soon to be VSCCA.

While Roy, Faro and Loucks were planting the seeds of a new beginning, an enthusiastic group of people were still racing pre-war, late 40's and early 50's sport cars in SCCA programs and other sanctioned events. At this time, many of these 'old' cars were becoming obsolete and non-competitive. Unfortunately, some cars found their way to junk piles or were left abandoned in garages to collect dust and mice. Others were rudely cut up for engine swaps or body modifications. Instead of giving up the thrill of competitive racing, some owners and drivers of these cars started to band together for the purpose of finding other ways to exercise their aging, mothballed sport cars.

Sports car racing in the streets of Aspen, Colorado—Circa 1952

Hence, in 1959, under the leadership of Roy and other disenchanted SCCA members, the first bonafide vintage racing organization - the VSCCA was officially founded on the East coast and in the Midwest. Another important 'happening' in the development of vintage racing took place at Elkhart Lake's Road America in Wisconsin, where 'old cars' of the past gathered for the first organized vintage race under the direction of the Inland Region of the VSCCA. Augie Pabst, a current participant in vintage racing, who runs several interesting vintage and historic cars, 'won' this inaugural race in 1959.

Throughout the decade of the 60's, the SCCA continued to experience an overwhelming growth in membership, while placing an increased emphasis on wheel-to-wheel competition. These trends caused negative feelings to develop within the rank and file of the SCCA, which led to different factions breaking away and forming their own racing organizations. In California, sports car enthusiasts who were unhappy with the SCCA, started looking elsewhere for the other venues to 'race' their old cars. Consequently, two California groups - the Classic Sports Racing Group (CSRG) and the Vintage Automobile Racing Association (VARA) were founded in the late 60's and early 70's, respectively.

In 1973, Steve Earle realized the potential of hosting a vintage racing event on the same weekend and in conjunction with the famous Pebble Beach Concours in Monterey, California. He gathered together some of his fellow auto enthusiasts and organized the Historic Motor Sports Association (HMSA) and the first Monterey Historic Races (MHR). Hence, some of the old cars that were sadly put out to pasture raced again with dignity on Monterey's Laguna Seca race track. The first Historic Race was a quaint, select gathering of vintage car enthusiasts who understood the value and *fun* of racing old cars.

Today, the Monterey Historic Races is the premier spectator vintage racing event in the world. In 1973, the first Historic's had only 80 cars in the paddock - this year (1989) over 1000 vintage and historic cars sought entry.

Vintage racing mirrors the same phenomenal growth the Monterey Historic Races has experienced over the years. Vintage racing groups, organizations and events have increased tremendously since the first MHR. The popularity of the sport has spread like wildfire across the U.S. and Canada.

In 1980, Florida's Southeast Vintage Racing Association staged its first race. Presently, the SVRA (now relocated to South Carolina and called the Sportscar Vintage Racing Association) has over 1000 members and is a consistent leader in spearheading the current popularity, growth and change that is now affecting the sport of vintage racing. Since the early 80's, other regional groups have formed, such as, the Vintage Sports Car Driver Association (VSCDA) out of Chicago, followed by the Rocky Mountain Vintage Racing (RMVR) from Denver. Currently, there are over 30 vintage racing organizations in the U.S. and Canada dedicated to the sport of racing old cars - with over 100 vintage racing events throughout the country that cover the entire calendar year. Although vintage racing organizations differ in policy and rules, the one common premise that pervades their philosophy is the restoration, preservation, racing and display of vintage cars, sport and spirit.

Vintage racing as a recreational activity has become a popular motorsport, not only in the U.S., but internationally as well. In England and Europe, the sport is considered to be highly competitive and requires a high standard of preparation and skill that sometimes borders on professionalism. A large, enthusiastic crowd is usually seen at most vintage races in England and on the Continent. The Europeans have always had a keen interest in motorsports, especially when it comes to racing old cars. Like Europe, the sport of vintage racing attracts a large following in the United States. Unlike some of our brethren across the pond, vintage racing in the U.S. is considered a gentleman's sport, where competition and the thrill of victory is secondary to a keen appreciation and love for vintage and historical automobiles.

A vintage race event in the U.S. is nothing more than a moving classic car show at speed with friendly competition thrown in as an added attraction. The cars and their history are the main headliners of the show. Unlike professional racing, the participants in vintage racing take a back seat as supporting players to the main character.

Vintage racing is an on-going theater production that awakens the dreams of our youth and rekindles the burning desire to own and drive the cars we once loved and cherished. In our younger days, many of us were unable to bring our dreams into reality. We were content watching the main objects of our desires and wondering how it would feel behind the wheel of one of those beautifully crafted, well engineered racing machines that stirred our emotions and raised our spirits. Some of us only have faded memories of our dreams and desires. Today, vintage racing has become a vehicle to re-live those wonderful experiences, faded memories and emotions of our youth.

There is something special in seeing and hearing the great marques of automotive racing history repeating their feats of glory on the same race tracks that once hosted sports car racing in its purest form.

Whatever reasons motivate you to own or race old cars, the vintage racing movement is cruising at top speed in high gear. Ca*t*ch the *Spirit*...!!

Augie Pabst, who won the first organized vintage car race in 1959 at Road America, drives his E-Type Jaguar Coupe on the same course during the 1989 VSCDA Vintage Fall Festival.

CHAPTER II

PREPARING YOURSELF

"preparation is the key to any successful endeavor"

Before seating yourself behind the wheel of a vintage race car, you need to prepare yourself mentally and physically. The act of racing cars, especially older cars can be very demanding and dangerous. Historically speaking, combining speed with the automobile has always been associated with many unfortunate experiences. Fortunately, in the United States vintage racing is, due to the nature of the sport, conducted under *controlled* conditions. Strict safety standards, a gentleman's attitude and less competition have helped to increase the degree of safety in vintage racing over and above professional racing.

The safety factor (SF) is constantly being monitored, emphasized and practiced - but on rare occasions accidents can happen. Within the last three to four years only two deaths have been attributed to vintage racing in the United States - both single car incidents caused by probable driver error. Understand that racing by its very nature, whether it be Formula One or Go-Karting is inherently dangerous to your health - ditto Vintage Racing. The degree of danger is relative to speed, driver attitude and safety standards. Before involvement in vintage racing, you must recognize the fact that although vintage racing is relatively safe, racing "old cars" can still affect your well-being. There have been instances of aspiring would be vintage racers displaying an overabundance of enthusiasm and discovering sadly that vintage racing was not for them.

Why? Unfortunately, their enthusiasm quickly turns to dismay and disillusion when they discover that racing can be dangerous and costly. An individual who accepts the risk of racing a car for money (professional) or recreation (vintage) needs to develop a certain mental toughness to overcome the unexpected that occasionally occurs when the combination of speed, asphalt and different driving abilities merge together. Accidents happen fast and furious on a race track - sometimes just by being in the wrong place at the wrong time. The possibility of having an accident when racing is not meant to scare or intimidate. It is important to understand and accept the risks involved in racing. Vintage racing is relatively a safe sport. The nature of the sport demands an increased awareness and judicial application of safety standards for car and driver. By allowing faster cars to pass, most vintage race participants strive to avoid confrontations and accidents.

Most participants compete in vintage racing primarily for the 'fun factor' - not for the win-at-all cost attitude that is prevalent in professional racing. A major philosophy behind a vintage event is not to win, but to *safely finish*. If you have a problem agreeing with or understanding this way of thinking, then you might be in the wrong sport. Augie Pabst, a well known veteran racer expresses a somewhat different point of view concerning the 'desire to win' attitude in vintage racing— he states, "although I am a strong believer in penalizing those racers who are reckless and lack proper judgment - anytime there is a race of any kind, human nature takes hold in that there will be some people who want to *win* and to think otherwise is a mistake. In our sport, we should accept this fact, but insist that any foolishness not be tolerated." Based on this philosophy, maybe the vintage race sponsors and organizers need to start devising separate race programs for the few people who want to drive their cars 'hard and fast' and have the overwhelming need to win. Nevertheless, the prevalent philosophy that exists in vintage racing today de-emphasizes the *desire to win* and *win-at-all cost* attitudes. Another important vintage racing philosophy is that the *car* is the main attraction - not the driver. If you have a big ego and want to race in heated wheel-to-wheel competition, you will probably find the Sports Car Club of America (SCCA) or International Motor Sports Association (IMSA) formats more suited to your needs. Vintage racing participants are interested mainly in enjoying their cars at speed and camaraderie with fellow competitors and vintage race car enthusiasts.

In addition to mental preparedness, there are physical demands placed on you when racing. Most vintage racing organizations require you to successfully complete a detailed physical, including an EKG and Urinalysis. Obviously, if a prospective candidate has heart, hormonal, sight, drug/alcohol or emotional problems - it is highly advised to look elsewhere for thrills and excitement. You need to assess your physical health. You should be in the best possible physical condition for your age group. Heart attacks can be lethal anywhere, especially on a race track. You place yourself in jeopardy as well as your fellow racers if you participate with known health problems.

An excellent method of assessing your values and assisting in answering questions concerning vintage racing is to attend racing events. Attend these events with the idea of acquiring as much information as possible. Talk to the drivers and ask them how they got started and prepared themselves for vintage racing. Look for other factors that might give you answers to your questions. An excellent avenue for acquiring first-hand knowledge about the vintage racing scene is to increase your involvement by becoming a crew member, corner worker or assisting in various behind-the-scene operations. There is a tremendous amount of energy and work required from people responsible for organizing and running race events. Race directors are always looking for volunteer help to assist with the race program. Many current vintage racers got their feet wet by volunteering as crew members or working as flaggers on the race track.

Another way of coming to terms with your capabilities in meeting the demands of vintage racing is to take part in a professional race driving course. Most vintage racing organizations require you to attend a recognized/acceptable race driving school. There are many excellent schools located around the country that cater to prospective race car drivers (see chapter V on schools). Vintage racing organizations usually offer their own version of driving schools. By successfully completing a course in race driving techniques, you will be able to better understand and evaluate your own capabilities and attitudes towards racing in general. In addition, if you continue in your pursuit of becoming a vintage race car driver, you would satisfy the requirement for a vintage competition license.

There is basically one major question to ask and answer before getting too deeply involved in vintage racing - *AM I MENTALLY PREPARED AND PHYSICALLY FIT?* Attending vintage race events in conjunction with a professional race driving course should help answer the above question.

If you can recognize and accept the inherent risks involved in racing and consider yourself in excellent physical health - you are now ready to select the main object of your desire - a vintage race car.

The 1965 Ford GT-40, #1026, driven by Gene Schiavone at the 1989 Chicago Historic Races.

CHAPTER III

SELECTING A VINTAGE RACE CAR

"the driving force in selecting a car for vintage racing depends on your goals, personal taste and financial status"

Vintage racing organizations have classified and grouped cars according to engine displacement, car type and year of manufacture. What follows is a partial list of cars currently being raced on vintage circuits. This list is based on general categories that are accepted by most vintage organizations. The purpose of this listing is to give you a general idea of what types of cars are eligible for competition.

VEHICLE CLASSIFICATION

GROUP A: Pre-war and early Post-war
GROUP B: Vintage I 1946-1959
                Class 1: Production Cars Under 2 Liter
                Class 2: Production Cars Over 2 Liter
                Class 3: Sports-Racing Cars Under 2 Liter
                Class 4: Sports-Racing Cars Over 2 Liter

GROUP C: Vintage II 1960-1963
                Class 1: Production Cars Under 2 Liter
                Class 2: Production Cars Over 2 Liter
                Class 3: Sports-Racing Cars Under 2 Liter
                Class 4: Sports-Racing Cars Over 2 Liter

GROUP D: All Monoposto Cars Through 1969
            Class 1: Front Engine Formula Junior
            Class 2: Rear Engine Formula Junior (early)
            Class 3: Rear Engine Formula Junior (late)
            Class 4: Formula Vee & Formula III 500cc
            Class 5: Formula I and II
            Class 6: Formula Ford

GROUP E: Historic I 1960-1973
            Class 1: Production Cars Under 2 Liter
            Class 2: Production Cars 2 to 3 Liter
            Class 3: Production Cars 3 to 5 Liter
            Class 4: Production Cars Over 5 Liter

GROUP F: Historic II 1960-1973
            Class 1: Prototype/Race Cars Under 2 Liter
            Class 2: Prototype/Race Cars 2 to 3 Liter
            Class 3: Prototype/Race Cars 3 to 5 Liter
            Class 4: Prototype/Race Cars Over 5 Liter

In most cases, cars in the Vintage Groups are large in number (production sport models), least expensive, readily available and easy to maintain. The Pre-War/Historic Groups conversely are usually rare, expensive, difficult to locate and maintenance heavy. The Monoposto Group are open-wheel single seaters with aluminum/fiberglass bodies on tube frames that were built for Formula type racing venues. They are readily available and relatively easy to maintain - especially the Formula Vee class which use early Volkswagen components.

An important consideration when selecting vintage machinery is to determine your personal taste and goals. Ask this important question - **WHAT DO I WANT FROM VINTAGE RACING?** Are you interested in headline status - a runner who is consistently in front of the pack or are you content to finish near the back of a race group? Answering these questions will help you determine the type of car to select for vintage racing.

For many vintage racing participants the only factor that motivates their involvement is the **fun factor**. Consequently, these people, commonly referred to as 'backpackers', are not interested in being numero uno on the false grid or finishing in the top ten. If you find yourself leaning towards the 'fun crowd' and the backpackers, then you would do fine selecting a car that is relatively fast, highly dependable, inexpensive to operate and a joy to drive on the track or street. If you have a strong need to own a 'fast', competitive vintage racer for the purpose of qualifying in the top five, then you need to re-evaluate your reasons for participating in vintage racing. There are other clubs and organizations that cater to your need to be in the limelight. On the other hand, if you desire to have a vintage racer that is fast, and you use the inherent speed in a safe manner, keeping in line with the spirit of vintage racing, then by all means go for the top ten finish and first slot on the false grid. But remember, much of the speed of any car comes from the driver's preparation and abilities (i.e. practice and schooling), so be prepared to invest in yourself as well.

Whatever road you take in selecting a race car, it is important to systematically evaluate all parts and components of your potential vintage racer - **BUYER BEWARE!!!** Many cars that are currently being advertised for sale on the vintage racing market have been updated or modified based on present day technology - so be aware of the vehicle that is portrayed as being stock and in "original condition", when in reality it might be totally unacceptable for vintage racing. In addition, there are many cars currently being offered for sale stating "vintage eligible" when in fact they are not. Your best bet is to check with the club or organization you plan to participate with <u>before</u> you purchase a "vintage eligible" car.

There are several national publications that advertise suitable vintage racers for purchase. VICTORY LANE magazine, a monthly publication, has an extensive listing of classic and historical race cars. Also, the bi-monthly glossy vintage racing magazine, VINTAGE MOTORSPORT has a classified selection of eligible cars. Another source for locating/buying a vintage race care is through auto clubs and organizations. For example,

if you were interested in running a classic Corvette, it would be worthwhile to join a national club that caters to Corvettes. The National Corvette Restorers Society (NCRS) publishes a classified section in their bi-monthly newsletter that lists a good selection of eligible cars. One of the best sources of locating your 'dream racer' is HEMMINGS MOTOR NEWS—a monthly publication that lists thousands of cars, marque by marque. HEMMINGS also has a separate category devoted to high performance autos and racers, plus other features you would find beneficial. Also, AUTOWEEK, the weekly auto news magazine has a classified section on vintage race cars.

Actually, the process of locating/selecting a vintage race car is fairly easy and uncomplicated. The outcome of your final choice is affected mainly by your own personal feelings and what you want from vintage racing. Many current participants selected their cars based on love for a certain marque or country, i.e. if you have German roots you might lean towards selecting a Porsche or VW powered Formula Vee. Some enthusiasts favor British iron, therefore they choose a racer that represents Queen Mary and the Union Jack. Word of caution—some aspiring vintage racers make the mistake of purchasing a car that is over and above their initial driving capabilities. It is highly recommended, unless you have had previous experience to avoid buying a car with excessive power to weight ratios. Most Cam-Am cars fit into this category. These cars were specifically built for high speed racing, consequently, it takes experience and knowledge to properly drive these cars in a safe manner. When learning how to swim, it is considered good practice to stay in the shallow end before venturing into deeper waters. Like swimming, begin with a racer that you know you can handle before progressing to more exotic vintage machinery.

Whatever vintage, classic or historic racer you select - GREAT TIMES ARE GUARANTEED!! You might not reap monetary rewards or news headlines, but you will be a *winner* just by competing and finishing.

One last thought—before purchasing your vintage racer, you need to insure that the frame, suspension, steering, wheels and brakes are in good to excellent working order. These are important safety items that are essential to your health and well-being. The condition of the engine and drivetrain are secondary to anything affecting your chances of longevity on this earth. Proper car preparation in conjunction with meeting safety standards are two important ingredients that insure your success in vintage racing. One without the other could result in tragic circumstances.

Curt Liposcak's beautifully prepared 1933 MG-J2. This car started and finished the 1989 cross-country Great America Race.

JAMES VYANSKI

CHAPTER IV

CAR PREPARATION & SAFETY

"kisss rule" - <u>K</u>EEP <u>I</u>T <u>S</u>AFE, <u>S</u>IMPLE AND <u>S</u>ANE

After you have acquired your vintage race car, the next phase in the process of obtaining your rookie stripes is making sure your car is properly prepared and made safe for racing. This phase can be rewarding or difficult, depending on your attitude towards vintage racing.

The *spirit* of vintage racing dictates that cars operate within their **original** configuration - allowing only period modifications. A straightforward example of a period modification would be switching stock SU carbs for high performance sidedraft DCOE Webers. Another example of a period modification would be milling the head to increase cylinder compression, while installing a high-lift camshaft made specifically for racing. Many sport production models of the 50's and 60's had these types of modifications done to increase street and track performance. The current trend in vintage racing is to protect **originality**. Vintage racing organizations are dictating that cars be maintained in their original form. New rules and regulations are being formulated and mandated in hopes of protecting originality. Hopefully, by enforcing these rules, the *spirit* of vintage racing will endure and survive.

Before the actual process of preparing your car, and to insure originality, you should review and become familiar with the specific rules that relate to your car. The best advice and guidance you can receive on originality and preparation is from you local vintage racing organization. They are the governing bodies that set the rules and perform technical inspections on race day. Know what type(s) of period modifications were allowed for your car back in the 'good ole days'. Some vintage racing organizations have gone to the extent of creating their own criteria for certain makes and models. The SVRA has formulated rules for the proper set-up of an Austin-Healey 3000 and is in the process of creating rules for other marques as well. Other vintage racing groups are following the same path as the SVRA in making sure that cars are prepared in their original configuration. It is important to inquire before preparing your car for vintage racing - it might save you time, energy, money and a lot of unneeded aggravation.

IMPROPER MODIFICATIONS DO NOT BELONG IN VINTAGE RACING. You cheat yourself, fellow competitors and the sport of vintage racing by not following proper guidelines. There have been cases of rookie and veteran vintage drivers, who sadly find themselves watching the featured race on Sunday from pit row, while their improperly prepared, "highly modified" sport racer collects dust on a trailer in the paddock - not fun and a wasted weekend at best. Remember, the only performance mods permitted are the type the car raced with back in its heyday. While it is OK to run with sidedraft Webers on a B series MGA engine, the vintage Gods would look unfavorably on a cut-up T series MG with the same engine and Webers. Word to the wise - check and double check to insure your car meets the stated requirements and is legal based on criteria set forth by your vintage racing organization. Avoid the embarrassment and hassle of showing up for tech with a car that is illegally full blown and not conforming to original specifications. Changing the original specs on a car changes its basic nature and character. The original car ceases to exist and becomes something totally different - a mere aberration of its former self. By following proper guidelines and protecting the originality of your car, you help foster the true *spirit* of vintage racing. Do not get caught with your pants down!!

As mentioned previously in Chapter Two, the safety factor (SF) is constantly being monitored by race officials. An important aspect of vintage racing and one that needs continued emphasis is that **safety** starts with *you* - the owner/driver. It is your responsibility to insure your vintage racer meets the basic safety requirements established by your vintage racing organization.

Through the history of auto racing there have been numerous unfortunate accidents caused by improper maintenance and defective components. Many racing participants make the mistake of spending an enormous amount of time and money restoring the engine and drivetrain, while neglecting the frame and suspension. There is little doubt that the condition of the engine and drivetrain are important to reliability and finishing the race - but does little to enhance the SF. Before anything is done in the preparation stage, the first and foremost step is to have the frame, chassis, steering and suspension components checked for faulty and weakened areas - especially where front-end parts connect to the frame. Defective or stressed suspension parts on old cars can cause unexpected havoc and disaster on a race track. Proper visual inspection and magufluxing of these areas will help insure nothing breaks loose unexpectedly at the wrong time. In addition, careful inspection and maintenance of these components will insure you finish the race with a pleasant smile and a good positive feeling. Spending your time in the paddock, sharing the camaraderie with fellow competitors after the race is more enjoyable than spending time behind a wrecking truck wondering what came unglued on turn five during the final lap.

Another area of importance and one worth mentioning before proceeding to the engine and drivetrain is to thoroughly inspect your car's braking system. Your brake system needs to be in excellent condition and capable of stopping your car at any speed. This does not mean replacing your car's legal drum brakes with illegal disc brakes because they stop your car quicker. Prepare your car's brake system to the best level possible within the rules of originality.

A driver during the 1986 Grand Bahama Vintage Grand Prix, had to scurry the entire town of Freeport to locate brake lines to replace his old, leaky rusted lines. Luckily, he discovered the leaks in the paddock while performing a routine oil change.

Can you imagine the possible consequences if the defective brake lines blew out in the heat of competition? Not only would this driver possibly shorten his life, but due to his lack of attention might have caused damage to his beautiful, rare 1959 Lancia Zagato Coupe. This incident should impress upon you the importance of checking and rechecking all car components that relate to safety on the track, especially your brake system.

When preparing vintage race cars, attention to detail is very important, especially safety related items. For racing purposes, a car that is bullet-proof **safe** pays better dividends then one that has a bullet-proof engine. Which car would you take if you wanted to finish the race in one piece?

So far, preparation and safety areas that you as a driver/owner have direct control have been dicussed. There are other areas of safety you need to know about and which you have very limited control. Most vintage racing organizations <u>require</u> the following minimum items:

A. DRIVER EQUIPMENT

1. HELMETS: All drivers should wear approved (1980 or later Snell Safety Foundation) helmet (1985 Snell strongly recommended).

2. CLOTHES: All drivers should wear an approved driving suit and underwear of flame retardant material, double layer Nomex or the equivalent.

3. FACE SHIELD: A protective face shield or goggles should be worn in all open cars and face shield or goggles in all closed cars is highly recommend.

B. CAR EQUIPMENT

1. SEAT BELTS: Cars should be equipped with a racing type seat belt 3" minimum and shoulder harness of nylon web (2" minimum) securely mounted to the frame of the car.

2. ROLL BAR: Properly built roll bars are required, except in competition exhibition (2" or more over the helmet).

3. FIRE EXTINGUISHERS: Cars should be equipped with a dry chemical fire extinguisher of at least 2 pounds (securely mounted into the cockpit).

In addition to the above, your car should have a firewall between the cockpit, engine and fuel tank. Catch tanks should be installed to prevent overflow of engine fluids. The suspension and steering should not have excessive wear or play. Your car should be fitted with at least one working brake light and have one rear view mirror. Leaks of any kind are prohibited. Your vintage racer's wheels should be in good condition, with even tension in the spokes, and no rust or corrosion at the spoke and/or rim.

The above is a general representation of what is required by most vintage racing organizations. You need to check with your particular organization to find out the full scope of what they require (see chapter on VROs). Some vintage organizations have different rules for attaching the roll bar and seat belts to the frame of the car. Vintage racing organizations are constantly changing and revamping their requirements for participation, so while inquiring about your car's originality, also ask about requirements concerning car and driver safety equipment.

It is up to the individual participants to see to it that their cars are in a safe race-worthy condition. Although a technical inspection of your car is conducted at the track, there is no way to ensure that safety defects would be discovered. Hence, the primary burden is on *you* to insure your car is in tiptop condition. Based on recommendations of the VINTAGE MOTORSPORTS COUNCIL (VMC), most vintage racing organizations have adopted the "13/13 Rule" to promote safety and etiquette. The rule states that any incident causing physical damage to a race car through contact with another race car or race track may result in suspension of the driver(s) involved from any further participation during the event depending on the determination of fault and circumstances. Any driver suspended from further participation will automatically be placed in a probationary status for the following 13 months. A similar infraction incurred while on probation will result in a 13 month period of ineligibility. Infractions resulting in disciplining actions are reported to other vintage racing organizations for review through the VMC. Avoid the **"13/13 Rule"** by maintaining your car to the highest possible standard of preparation and safety. Then <u>drive</u> to that standard. This is the key to getting the most enjoyment from vintage racing.

The question that always needs to be asked is: **AM I ENJOYING MYSELF?** All aspects of vintage motorsports should be enjoyable, and you should be able to say yes quickly to the above question. It has been suggested that drivers wear open-faced or transparent helmets, so that those not smiling can be black flagged. When all the serious aspects are integrated into the whole, the grin should remain.

Westport Photoracing—Mike Farley

CHAPTER V

DRIVING SCHOOLS

"you have an obligation to yourself and other competitors to learn the proper methods of driving safely at speed"

Before participation in any auto racing event - vintage or other, it is mandatory to attend a recognized driving school. The major reason vintage racing organizations require you to successfully complete a race driving school is to insure that you develop the necessary skills and competency to drive fast at a safe speed. There are several professional driving schools located across the country. Each offers expert instruction, driving techniques and advice. Some schools give courses, from beginner to advanced levels, based on the student's experience and skill. Attending and completing a professional driving school is an excellent way to satisfy the licensing requirement set forth by most vintage racing organizations.

Another option and one that should be considered is to attend a driving school offered by your local vintage racing organization. For example, the VSCDA conducts their own qualifying drivers' school early in the season (April-May) at Blackhawk Farms Raceway outside of Chicago. These schools are usually well attended by club members. Veteran drivers use these schools to re-sharpen their driving skills in preparation for the upcoming season. Besides having a good mix of veteran and rookie drivers on hand, these schools are low key and are staffed by experienced senior members of the organization. The veteran vintage racers who attend these driving schools are usually more than happy to offer their expertise and advice in assisting the rookie driver. It is an excellent opportunity for a beginner to observe and take note how these seasoned drivers ply their skill. An ample amount of track and classroom time is allotted for the neophyte racer to acquire the basic skills of on-track race car driving. Occasionally, as an added attraction and to assist in the learning of driving skills, guest instructors are hired to teach and give advice. These visiting head instructors are usually of world class caliber and readily available to offer assistance and advice on the finer points of high speed driving techniques.

Another method of satisfying the vintage racing organization school requirement, while sharpening your skills is to attend a driving school offered in conjunction with a vintage racing event. In most cases, the sponsoring organization arranges a contract with the host race track to provide track and classroom instruction on the days preceeding the main weekend racing event. Most major race tracks employ a professional staff that is responsible for the operation of the driving school. Based on this approach, you could attend driving school during the week and race on the very same weekend - provided you pass the driving course.

There are many people who participate in two or more driving schools before actually competing on the track. This deliberate approach, as compared to the "school one day, race next day" method, allows you to gradually get acquainted with your car and your limitations on the track.

The amount of time and preparation spent on developing driving skills depends on your individual goals and budget. A good rule of thumb, and one that is practiced by most aspiring vintage drivers is to attend as many driving schools as needed until you feel the confidence and ability to handle the demands of race car driving. The more instruction and track time you get under your belt before actual competition, the more you will be prepared for the rigors of racing. Knowing yourself and performance capabilities of your car are probably the most important factors in establishing your credibility as a bonafide vintage race car driver.

There are many avenues to take in satisfying the licensing requirement for vintage racing. It would help if you would take the time and effort to do a little research before arbitrarily attending a driving school. You will find the professional schools more expensive compared to courses given by your local organizations. However, the time and money spent on a professional school is well worth what you receive in return and the final results. Schools given by your local organizations are not quite as sophisticated or involved as the professional schools, but do an excellent job in preparing you for vintage racing. Many vintage racing organizations require you to take part in a professional driving school as well as their local driving school.

Whatever method you decide in obtaining the skills and knowledge on high speed driving techniques - remember to be serious in your endeavor to learn as much as possible about yourself, your car and racing in general.

contact the following professional driving schools and your local racing organizations for further information

DRIVING SCHOOLS

Akin-White Racing School
4320 W. Osborne Ave.
Tampa, Florida 33614
(813)874-5944

Skip Barber Racing School
RT. 7, Bldg. C
Canaan, CT. 06018
(203)824-0771

High Performance Road Racing Course
Road Atlanta, Rt. 1
Braselton, GA. 30517
(404)967-6143

Jim Russell British School of Motor Racing
P.O. BOX 119 AC-6
Mt. Tremblant, Quebec, Canada J0T-1Z0
(819)425-2739

Bondurant School of High Performance Driving
Sears Point International Raceway
Hwy. 37 & 121
Sonoma, CA. 95476
(707)938-4741

Bertil Roos School of High Performance Driving
P.O. BOX 221A
Blakeslee, PA. 18610
(717)646-7227

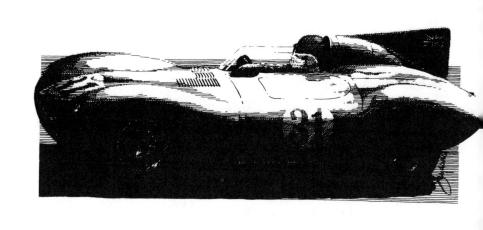

CHAPTER VI

VINTAGE RACING ORGANIZATIONS (VRO'S)

"even though vintage racing organizations differ in policy and rules, the one common premise that pervades their philosophy is the restoration, preservation, racing and display of vintage cars, sport and spirit"

GENERAL VINTAGE RACING RULES & REGULATIONS

The below <u>GENERAL</u> vintage racing rules and regulations apply to most vintage racing organizations - you need to check with your local VRO for specific details.

I. VEHICLE PREPARATION

A. BODY

1. The body configuration will be as raced in year of manufacture. Supplemental aerodynamic devices such as spoilers, air dams and wings are not permitted. Fender flares and/or fender widening are not permitted on Vintage Production cars. Fender flares may be permitted on Historic Production cars if the car raced in the configuration in the year of production. It is up to the entrant to substantiate any deviation in the body configuration of the car.

2. Interiors will be neat and finished. Vintage production cars must have the original dashboard in place. Supplementary gauges are allowed but must be neatly mounted. Drivers seats may be replaced with a racing type seat. Passenger seats are optional. Floorboard carpeting must be removed.

3. All exterior trim items including grill must be in place on production cars. Production cars may blank off the headlight openings. Headlight openings may not be used for ducting air. Bumpers may be removed. Nerf bars are prohibited.

4. Brake ducts are permitted but may not be visible from outside the car.

B. WHEELS

1. Wheels may vary 10% in diameter from what was originally fitted in the year of production. Standard wheel widths may be increased by 1″ or a homologated wheel width may be used. Period looking after market wheels will be for cars originally fitted with 12 inch wheels which may change to 13 inch wheels and cars originally fitted with metric sizes (380mm and 400mm) which may change to 16 inch wheels (not all VRO's have adopted this rule.)

C. TIRES

CHECK WITH LOCAL VRO FOR RULES & REGS ON TIRES

D. ENGINE

The entrant must with certainty disclose the correct engine displacement. Engines must be of the original type and design as **originally** fitted by the manufacturer. The following engine modifications are specifically prohibited on **production based cars**:

1. Wet sump oiling system may not be converted to dry sump.

2. The fuel induction system must be as provided by the manufacturer. Carburetors may not be changed to fuel injection or vice versa.

3. The method of valve actuation: lifters, tappets and rocker arms must be as manufactured. Roller lifters, roller cams and roller rocker arms are prohibited unless originally fitted by the manufacturer. Period aftermarket heads are allowed. Modern aftermarket heads and blocks are prohibited. Blocks and heads must be of the same material as provided by the manufacturer.

4. Transmissions must be provided by the manufacturer. Reverse must work and be selectable by the driver when seated. Aftermarket transmissions are prohibited. Gear ratios are free.

E. SUSPENSION

The system of suspension: spring type and number, shock-absorber type and number may not be changed and must be attached to the factory mountings.

CHECK WITH LOCAL VRO FOR RULES & REGS ON SUSPENSION

F. BRAKES

Braking system must be the same type as was standard for the year of manufacture or was homologated by the original manufacturer. Updating or backdating among a range of production years is prohibited.

CHECK WITH LOCAL VRO FOR RULES & REGS ON BRAKES

G. OTHER

1. All oil, fuel, water and brake lines must be secure and free of leaks. Catch cans to receive any possible overflow or blow-by from engine, radiator or transmission are mandatory.

2. All cars must have at least one brake light in working order.

3. All cars must have mirrors fitted which provide the driver visibility rearward and on both sides of the car.

4. Hoods, deck lids, doors and other body components must be securely fastened.

5. Batteries must be securely mounted with a metal hold-down. The hot terminal must be insulated to prevent accidental grounding.

6. Competition numbers must be displayed legibly and neatly (check with local VRO for specific details).

II. SAFETY RECOMMENDATIONS

A. SEAT BELTS

All cars will be equipped with a SCCA or IMSA standard five or six point driver restraint system. In all cases the system must consist of a 3" wide lap belt and 2 " wide over the shoulder harness. All straps will be in excellent condition and securely attached.

B. ROLL BARS

CHECK WITH LOCAL VRO FOR RULES & REGS ON ROLL BARS

C. FIRE EXTINGUISHERS

All cars will be equipped with a dry chemical or halon fire extinguisher of at least 2 lbs. securely mounted in the cockpit within driver's reach.

D. CUT-OFF SWITCH

An electrical cut-off switch is required on all cars (optional in some VRO's). Such switch shall be clearly marked from the outside of the car and disconnect all electrical components from the power source.

III. DRIVER EQUIPMENT

A. HELMETS

It is recommended all drivers wear an automobile racing helmet of 1985 or later Snell approval or equivalent. Helmets of 1980 approval are required. Full face helmets are required for all open cockpit cars. All drivers will wear adequate eye protection.

B. SUITS

All drivers must wear a suit that covers the body from the neck to the wrist and ankles; be made of fire resistant material(Nomex, Durette, ect.); and be worn with fire resistant underwear. All drivers must wear gloves, shoes and socks of fire resistant material(gloves and shoes may be leather). Drivers with facial hair or exposed hair must wear fire resistant hoods.

IV. MEDICAL EXAMINATION

All drivers must file an approved competition medical form every two years. Evidence of having provided an acceptable medical form with another racing body will be accepted.

V. TECHNICAL INSPECTION

A technical inspection will be conducted on all cars at events. It is the owner/entrant's responsibility to know the car is in safe working order. **All items in these rules may be checked with a special emphasis on safety.** All cars must be in good condition and display care in preparation. Driver safety gear must be presented at tech inspection. **THE CHIEF OF TECH MAY REJECT ANY ENTRY.**

VI. CONDUCT

All drivers are subject to the **13/13 RULE** which states: if you are at fault in an incident which causes damage to your car or anyone elses car, you are out of that event and on probation for 13 months. Any further incidents while on probation will result in suspension for 13 months. Any car involved in a crash, or having contact with another car sufficient to produce body, frame or suspension damage is automatically withdrawn from the event (not all VRO's have this rule).

VINTAGE RACING ORGANIZATIONS

*ARIZONA SPORTS RACING ASSOCIATION (ASRA)

A. ADDRESS: ASRA
c/o John Baker
4446 E. Shomi St.
Phoenix, AZ 85044
(602) 893-3463

B. HISTORY: ASRA was formed in 1962 by six people who just wanted to race without all the hassles imposed by other race groups. ASRA has grown to about 150 members, including wives and other workers, and has about 75 cars at regular monthly events.

C. PHILOSOPHY: Vintage racing should be fun and safe with special emphasis placed on the restoration and preservation of classic race cars.

D. LICENSE: Drivers must be a holder of a competition license from a recognized racing organization (i.e. RMVR, VARA, SCCA, ASRA, ect.)

E. CAR ELIGIBILITY: The following type designations will be eligible:
1.   Production sports cars (thru 1967).
2.   Selected sports sedans (thru 1967).
3.   Sports racing cars (thru 1972).
4.   Formula cars (thru 1972).
5.   Historic & Factory Prototype cars (thru 1967).
6.   Selected exhibition cars (Can-Am, Indy, thru 1972).

F. MEMBERSHIP: All entrants of an ASRA event must be members of ASRA. Annual dues are $50.00 and race entries vary from $100.00 to $175.00.

G. OTHER: ASRA runs its own driving school. ASRA will accept some older cars with modifications for safety reasons that the purist clubs do not accept. Major race event is held at Firebird Raceway near Phoenix in February.

HISTORIC MOTOR SPORTS ASSOCIATION (HMSA)

HISTORIC MOTOR SPORTS ASSOCIATION

P.O. Box 30628, Santa Barbara, California 93130-0349

A. ADDRESS: HMSA
c/o Debbie Donovan
P.O. BOX 30628
Santa Barbara, CA 93130
(805) 966-9151 FAX 805-966-5028

B. HISTORY: Originally founded by Steve Earle in 1973. Sponsor of the Monterey Historic Races.

C. PHILOSOPHY: The purpose of HMSA is to encourage the restoration, preservation and use of historic, sports and racing cars. HMSA events are not meant to be another category of real racing or a haven for the warriors from SCCA, IMSA, and NASCAR. HMSA places a very heavy emphasis on the driver. He is responsible for the preparation and safe operation of the car.

D. LICENSE: A racing license is not required. However, drivers must present evidence of experience in the form of one of the following:

    1. A current competition license issued by the FIA or an ACCUS member (SCCA, IMSA).

    2. Evidence of the satisfactory completion of a full course in competition driving from a recognized driving school and a resume of experience.

    3. A resume of experience listing previous races and vintage events run, types of cars driven, licenses held in the past, current vintage licenses and driving record.

E. CAR ELIGIBILITY:

CLASS A

A-1	1900-1926	Sports & Racing Cars.
A-2	1927-1939	Sports Cars.
A-3	1929-1939	Racing Cars.

CLASS B

B-1	1947-1955	Sports Cars (GT).
B-2	1947-1955	Sports Racing Cars under 1500cc.
B-3	1947-1955	Sports Racing Cars over 1500cc.

CLASS C

C-1	1955-1960	Sports Racing Cars under 2000cc.
C-2	1955-1959	Sports Racing Cars over 2000cc.

CLASS E

E-1	1950-1957	Formula I-II.
E-2	1958-1963	Formula I-II.
E-3	1958-1963	Formula Jr.

CLASS G
    G-1   1955-1961 GT Cars under 2000cc.
    G-2   1956-1962 GT Cars over 2000cc.
    G-3   1962-1965 GT Cars under 2000cc.
    G-4   1963-1965 GT Cars over 2000cc.

CLASS I
    1965-1972 FIA Makes Championship Cars.

F. MEMBERSHIP: Yearly dues are $50.00, which includes a subscription to Vintage Motorsport Magazine.

G. OTHER: Any driver in an accident sufficient to cause damage will be excluded from any future event. He may appeal exclusion after one years time from the date of the incident. Major race event is the Monterey Historics at Leguna Seca Raceway in August.

*ROCKY MOUNTAIN VINTAGE RACING (RMVR)

A. ADDRESS: RMVR
                 c/o Karen Nichols
                 61 Golden Eagle Lane
                 Littleton, CO. 80127
                 (303) 933-1207

B. HISTORY: Denver based, Rocky Mountain Vintage Racing, has over 600 members who are dedicated to the restoration, preservation and racing of vintage cars. RMVR, founded in 1982 with only 7 members, has grown to become one of the most active race clubs in the United States.

C. PHILOSOPHY: The primary objective of the sport of vintage and historic automobile racing is to promote the preservation of these cars in a racing format which emphasizes driver safety and etiquette. The sport is intended to provide a format for friendly wheel to wheel competition with vehicles prepared faithfully to their era. All racing is dangerous and only the proper attitude of the driver and the careful preparation of cars will diminish the danger and enhance our appreciation of this sport.

D. LICENSE:
 1. Applicants 18 - 21 yrs. old.

   a. Applicants must have successfully completed a recognized drivers school or hold a competition license.

   b. Applicants must participate in two (2) RMVR racing events, and meet with the approval of the chief driving instructor.

 2. Applicants 21 yrs. and older:

   a. Applicants must successfully complete one (1) RMVR drivers school.

   b. **Or** - have completed a recognized drivers school, or hold a current competition license, or current vintage racing license from another VRO.

c. Applicants must participate in two (2) racing events, and/or meet with the approval of the chief driving instructor.

E. CAR ELIGIBILITY:
1. Production sport cars thru 1967.
2. Selected sports sedans thru 1967.
3. Sports racing cars thru 1972.
4. Historic and factory prototype thru 1967.
5. Formula cars thru 1972.
6. Selected exhibition cars thru 1972.

F. MEMBERSHIP: Membership dues are $35.00 per year due and payable on or before January 1st of each year. All entrants of an RMVR event must be members of RMVR.

G: OTHER: The calendar year is full of scheduled events planned throughout Colorado, including street races and the premier event in Steamboat Springs in September. RMVR also uses Mountain View Racetrack located NW of Denver for some of its events. The official publication of RMVR is a bi-monthly news magazine called THE APEX. You need not own a vintage car to become a member and participate in RMVR.

SOCIETY OF VINTAGE RACING ENTHUSIASTS (SOVREN)

A. ADDRESS: SOVREN
c/o Donna Thorson (President)
18820 S.E. 42nd St.
Issaquah, WA 98027
(206) 641-3551

B. HISTORY: SOVREN was founded in 1985 and incorporated as a non-profit organization in 1986.

C: PHILOSOPHY: SOVREN's approach to the sport is for the restoration, preservation and friendly competition of vintage and historical automobiles - "old friends playing with old cars".

D: LICENSE: A license or proven proficiency is required. All members should obtain a CASC, SCCA, or IRDC license.

E: CAR ELIGIBILITY: Eligibility rules are for cars in an as raced configuration prior to 12/31/69. There are 3 (three) general groups: 1) Pre-War 2) Vintage - manufactured prior to 12/31/61 3) Historic - manufactured before 12/31/69. The basis for this eligibility break off is the massive technology change that happened to tires and aerodynamics as well as the change in approach to racing about this time. The early 70's was when racing ceased to be a sport and became an industry.

F: MEMBERSHIP: Dues are $30.00 per year with a $10.00 initiation fee.

G: OTHER: SOVREN requires roll bars which must be above the drivers' heads, five-point harnesses, 1980 or better helmets and Nomex or equivalent drivers suit (2 layers plus underwear), gloves and shoes.

*SPORTSCAR VINTAGE RACING ASSOCIATION
(SVRA)

A: ADDRESS: SVRA
2725 W. 5th North St.
Summerville, SC 29483
(803) 871-3430

B: HISTORY: The SVRA was founded in 1980. Originally based in Florida under the name Southeast Vintage Racing Association, the SVRA has grown in numbers and stature since 1980. Presently membership is well over 1000 and growing. The SVRA sponsors and sanctions 12 vintage racing events throughout the year.

C: PHILOSOPHY: SVRA intends to promote the historical preservation and use of racing sports cars and to create a spirit of safety consciousness among its members with an atmosphere of friendly competition at events. The object is to present a program for well prepared cars faithful to their period and to recreate a lost era in motorsport. Appearance of the car and authenticity of configuration is vital. Vintage racing is an amateur sport where the pleasure of "taking part" must exceed the desire to "win at all cost". All competitors must know the limits of their skills and the limits of their machines.

D: LICENSE: Drivers will present evidence of having successfully completed an approved professional drivers' school or be a current license holder of a recognized racing organization. Certain cars may require SVRA to request more detailed driver qualifications and/or additional experience.

E: CAR ELIGIBILITY:

1. Vintage: Race cars constructed prior to 12/31/59.
Production based sports cars to 12/31/62.
Makes 1955-1967 under 1300cc - small bore.
2. Historic: Race cars constructed and raced prior to 12/31/72.
Production based sports cars 1/1/63 to 12/31/67.
Selected FIA GT and Trans-Am to 12/31/72.
3. Formula: Formula 1 through 1965; Formula Junior (1100cc) through 1964; other Formula cars through 12/31/59. The following are not eligible: Ford; Vee; 1960 or later: B; C; Two; Three; Four; Continental; 5000; Libre; USAC. NOTE: The Formula Vee class may be eligible in 1990 (check with SVRA).

F. MEMBERSHIP: Yearly membership:

1. Driver - $60.00
2. General Membership - $50.00

G. OTHER: SVRA has established for certain cars a list of specs and preparation standards (inquire). Approved fuel cells and roll bars are required for all cars. Split (2 circuit) master brake cylinders are required. SVRA conducts its own drivers' school and test day in February at Roebling Road near Savannah, Georgia. It sponsors vintage events at the following race tracks: Moroso, Sebring, Memphis, Mid-Ohio, Road Atlanta, Summit Point, plus vintage racing in the Bahamas in January.

*CLASSIC SPORTS RACING GROUP (CSRG)

CSRG

A. ADDRESS: CSRG
P.O. BOX 488
Los Altos, CA. 94023
(415) 948-2857

B. HISTORY: The Classic Sports Racing Group was founded in 1968. Its members are enthusiasts dedicated to the preservation and use of sports racing and formula automobiles.

C. PHILOSOPHY: Simply stated, it is the policy and purpose of CSRG to provide race track events for its members. These events are for historic racing and selected production cars maintained in their original condition as nearly as possible and used in a sportsmanlike context that accommodates widely varying track skills and driver experience. The CSRG represents an attitude that has much to do with the appreciation, preservation and use of the car and relatively little to do with conventional racing that defines the car as a tool with which to win at all costs. CSRG does not and will not discourage competition, provided it is done with safety and with respect for one's fellow driver. Historic racing, as defined in CSRG is different from other forms of racing in that it is based upon participation, not victory. **THE RACER WHOSE ONLY PURPOSE IS WINNING HAS NO PLACE IN THE CSRG STRUCTURE.**

D. LICENSE: Formal licensing is replaced by mutual respect for each other's rights. A yearly drivers' clinic is held in which the experienced drivers help the beginners to improve their skills. (check with CSRG for further info).

E. CAR ELIGIBILITY:

1. Pre-1962 Historic Sports Racing Cars.
2. Certain Pre-1962 Approved Formula Cars.
3. Formula Junior Cars.
4. Rare and Unusual G.T. Cars.
5. Pre-1949 European Sports Cars.
6. Selected Production Cars through 1962.
7. 1962-1965 Sports Racing Cars under 2 Liter.

F. MEMBERSHIP: Annual dues are $25.00.

G. OTHER: CSGR events are held at Sears Point Raceway near Sonoma, California. Medical cards from other VRO are usually accepted. CSRG encourages members to take advantage of all available safety precautions and equipment.

VINTAGE MOTORCAR RACING (VMR)

A. ADDRESS: VMR
1800 Market St., #20
San Francisco, CA. 94102
(415) 364-8855

B. PHILOSOPHY: Vintage Motorcar Racing is an organization which offers opportunities to those who have restored or preserved historic GT, production, sport racing and formula cars to enjoy their vehicles by driving them safely and skillfully at speed on safe road racing circuits. Participation and enjoyment are basic to VMR events. Winning is secondary.

C. LICENSE: A participant must be a current SCCA member to drive VMR events. A SCCA vintage, regional or national racing license is required to participate in VMR events. Valid competition licenses from other recognized sanctioning bodies may also be accepted. SCCA vintage license can be issued based on previous experience, either racing or driver training, at the discretion of VMR.

D: CAR ELIGIBILITY:

    1.   Small displacement production cars through 1969.
    2.   Small displacement sports racing and GT cars through 1969.

3. Large displacement production cars through 1969.
4. Large displacement sports racing and GT cars through 1969.
5. FIA makes championship cars through 1969.
6. Formula cars through 1969.
7. Exhibition cars, including Can-AM, Formula-1 and others.

E. MEMBERSHIP: $30.00 annual fee.

F: OTHER: VMR has 3 vintage racing events scheduled throughout the calendar year. In addition, they sponsor their own drivers' school at Sears Point Raceway in January & February. VMR's main vintage event is the annual Fall Classic the last weekend in October at Sears Point. There are approximately 300 member/competitors in VMR.

*VINTAGE SPORTS CAR CLUB OF AMERICA
(VSCCA)

VINTAGE SPORTS CAR CLUB
OF AMERICA, INC.

170 WETHERILL ROAD
GARDEN CITY, NEW YORK 11530

A. ADDRESS: VSCCA
170 Wetherill Rd.
Garder City, NY 11530
(914) 234-6494

B. HISTORY: VSCCA was formed in 1959. It has the distinction of being the oldest VRO. The club is unique in its choice of eligible cars in that each car proposed must be passed by a classification committee which decides if the car is rare and/or unusual enough to be added to the list of homologated machines. All members share one common characteristic - a love for the beauty and excitement of running vintage cars.

C: PHILOSOPHY: The primary purpose of the club is to encourage the acquisition, preservation and restoration of vintage sports cars; also to act as a source of technical information, and to establish rules and regulations covering all activities of the club.

D. LICENSE: VSCCA has no license requirement. However, new members are required to attend the VSCCA drivers' school and they are then observed for the next two events.

E. CAR ELIGIBILITY:

ELIGIBLE POST-WAR CARS

Class I - small cars (2 litres and under) from 1945-1959

    a.   Sports cars.
    b.   Formula cars.
    c.   Formula junior cars.

Class II - large cars (2 litres and over) from 1945-1959

    a.   Sports cars.
    b.   Formula cars.

Class III - rare and unusual sports cars and race cars of historical significance made in limited numbers from 1945-1959 and deemed excessively powerful and therefore eligible under Class I. Note: Eligibility of these cars for VSSCA events are limited by by-laws (check with VSCCA for additional information).

ELIGIBLE PRE-WAR CARS

Class I - sports cars and race cars (2 litres and under) built before 1945.

Class II - sports cars and race cars (2 litres and over) built before 1945.

F. MEMBERSHIP: active membership - $55.00; this annual fee includes annual dues, initiation fee and car badge.

G. OTHER: VSCCA has very strict car eligibility rules. Lime Rock RaceWay, located in Connecticut, is considered home for the VSCCA. In addition to friendly wheel-to wheel competition, VSCCA sponsors time trials and hillclimbs (Mt. Equinox in Vermont)

VINTAGE RACING CLUB OF BRITISH COLUMBIA
(VRCBC)

A. ADDRESS: VRCBC
5898 Crescent Dr.
Delta, B.C. CANADA
V4K 2E9
(604) 946-1545

B. HISTORY: VRCBC was started in 1976. It is the oldest VRO in Canada and the first club north of San Francisco. A small number of Vancouver area enthusiasts formed the club that was conceived as a means of sharing with others who, like themselves, loved to drive and experience those incredible racing machines of bygone days.

C. PHILOSOPHY: The stated purpose of the VRC of BC is to restore, race and exchange information, stock and parts concerning vintage sports and racing automobiles. Its members are dedicated to the preservation and enjoyment of antique and vintage sports and racing cars that are such an important part of our heritage.

D. LICENSE: In order to participate in VRCBC events, you need to attend a 2 day CASC (Canadian Automobile Sports Club) driver training school, or bring a current CASC license and apply for a vintage license. For USA drivers, either a current SCCA license or a letter from the individual's VRO stating that he/she is an experienced vintage driver.

E. CAR ELIGIBILITY:

CLASSES:
    1. Pre-war (built prior to 1940)
        a. Including all 'T' series MG's.

2. Post-war
   a. Monoplace, sports, sports-racing, series-production grand touring and special GT cars built between 1941-1961.
   b. Also includes cars built after the above date, of a continuing and unchanged model, conforming to the 1961 specifications, as long as the particular vehicle was built prior to 1970 and the model type has been out of production for at least 10 years.

3. Historic
   a. Sports racing cars built between 1962-1964.
   b. Formula junior cars built before 1962.

4. Limited Production
   a. Sports, grand touring prototypes made for competition purposes only, manufactured prior to 1970 and that have been out of production for not less that 10 years.

5. Other
   a. VRC of BC lists other eligible cars that do not fall into the above categories - please inquire for additional information.

F. MEMBERSHIP: You do not need to own a car to be a member of VRCBC. The only requirement is a sincere interest in vintage cars. Annual dues are $Cdn 40.00 for a single member, $Cdn 50.00 for a family membership.

G. OTHER: VRCBC has approximately 128 members, most of

whom reside in British Columbia and Washington State, and average more than two vintage cars per member. The club's main event is its annual Historic Weekend, usually held in early July at Westwood, near Cogvitlam, BC.

*VINTAGE SPORTS CAR RACING (VSCR)

A. ADDRESS: VSCR
                8108 ll5th Ln. N.
                Champlin, MN 55316
                (612) 427-9416

B. HISTORY: VSCR was formed in 1975 to provide a means to arrange for track time so that vintage sports car enthusiasts could run their cars at speed. The first race was held during the Trans Am weekend at Brainerd International Raceway in 1976. In 1983, the club began renting the track for vintage-only events, and that continued until 1987 when track dates became unavailable. Since then, VSCR has run vintage/historic races in conjunction with the SCCA regional races at Brainerd.

C. PHILOSOPHY: VSCR's philosophy is to provide track time to run vintage sports and race cars wheel to wheel, while maintaining a high degree of safety. This is reinforced by not allowing trophies, points or prize money.

D. LICENSE: Drivers must have completed one driving school, or show prior competition experience, or possess a competition driving license from another club. An SCCA vintage license is required to race in SCCA sanctioned vintage races.

E. CAR ELIGIBILITY: Vintage sports and racing cars thru 1962 and Formula Juniors thru 1963; Historic cars are all sports and racing cars, select FIA GT, select Tran-Am and select sports sedans 1963 thru 1972; all Formula Vees thru 1970 and other wheel Formula cars thru 1970.

F. MEMBERSHIP: Membership is open to any vintage/historic car enthusiasts. Annual dues are $25.00, which covers the club newsletter, monthly meetings, regalia and trackside parties.

G. OTHER: VSCR holds monthly general membership meetings, has two test days at local airports each season and races at Brainerd International Raceway 3-4 times each season.

*VINTAGE AUTOMOBILE RACING ASSOCIATION OF CANADA (VARAC)

A. ADDRESS: VARAC
                c/o Ed Delong
                3300 Yonge St., Suite 202
                Toronto, Ontario M4N 2L6

B. HISTORY: VARAC was formed in 1976 in order to organize race meetings for sports and race cars built prior to the end of 1961 and to provide a central organizing body through which vintage race enthusiasts could communicate with each other.

C. PHILOSOPHY: The spirit of VARAC can be expressed as a wish to preserve, restore and race historically significant cars in a form as close to the original specifications as possible. The aim of the club is to run races in the style of the 50's and 60's i.e. good fun racing, rather than the ultra-competitive racing found in events for current race cars.

D. LICENSE: It is a requirement for Canadian residents that they are members of a CASC affiliated club such as VARAC. With a current CASC race license and a road driver's license they are then able to enter races anywhere in Canada and the United States. A vintage license from any major U.S. vintage racing organization is acceptable for VARAC events.

E. CAR ELIGIBILITY:
  1. Pre-war cars.
  2. Post-war single seaters and formula juniors.
  3. Post-war production sports cars.
  4. Post-war sports racing cars.
  5. Classic sedans.
  6. Historic sports racing cars.
  7. Historic production sports cars.

F. MEMBERSHIP: Yearly membership is:
   1. $50.00 (Canadian)
   2. $45.00 (U.S.)

G. OTHER: The high point for VARAC is the Vintage Racing Festival. VARAC members enter numerous races promoted by organizations south of the border. All these events result in travel to new places and making new friends - an important and enjoyable aspect of the whole spectrum of vintage racing.

*VINTAGE SPORTS CAR DRIVER ASSOCIATION (VSCDA)

 VINTAGE SPORTS CAR DRIVERS ASSOCATION Ltd.

A. ADDRESS: VSCDA
                c/o John Kleen
                BOX C, 15 W. Burton Pl.
                Chicago, IL. 60610
                (312) 787-7838

B. HISTORY: Formed in late 1978 by members of the Prairie Region of the VSCCA. VSCDA held its first event in April of 1979. Since 1985, VSCDA has hosted the Elkhart Lake Vintage Festival on the first weekend in October at Road America, and since 1987 the Vintage Grand Prix au Grattan in Michigan. Membership is around 400.

C. PHILOSOPHY: The preservation through use of sports cars of 'that certain age'; and the encouragement of this use through friendly and appropriate competition.

D. LICENSE: License not required of members in club events, but drivers must have attended VSCDA drivers'school, and have shown appropriate ability. Non-members must offer documentation of driving competence; VMC license preferred.

E. CAR ELIGIBILITY:
   1. Pre-war and early Post-war
   2. Vintage I (1946-1959)
     a. Production cars over & under 2 liters.
     b. Sport-racing cars over & under 2 liters.

   3. Vintage II (1960-1963)
     a. Production cars over & under 2 liters.
     b. Sport-racing cars over & under 2 liters.

   4. Monoposto (through 1963)
     a. Front engine formula junior.
     b. Rear engine formula junior.
     c. Formula vee & formula III (500cc).
     d. Formula I and II.
     e. Formula ford.

   5. Historic I (1960-1973)
     a. Production cars under & over 2 liters.

   6. Historic II (1960-1973)
     a. Prototype/race cars under & over 2 liters.

F. MEMBERSHIP: Open to all interested enthusiasts - $25.00 per year; $30.00 for memberships including spouse.

G. OTHER: Charter member of VMC; members involved in founding of the Monoposto Register; drivers' school at Black-hawk Farms.

IMPORTANT: THE ABOVE INFORMATION ON VINTAGE RACING ORGANIZATIONS WAS COMPILED BASED ON INFORMATION SENT TO THE AUTHOR BY THE INDIVIDUAL ORGANIZATIONS AND WAS ACCURATE TO 1990.

Indicates membership in the VINTAGE MOTORSPORTS COUNCIL

OTHER VINTAGE RACING CLUBS & ORGANIZATIONS

CLASSIC AUTOMOBILE RACING ENTHUSIASTS (CARE)*
3010 SW 14th Pl., Unit 12 & 13
Boynton Beach, FL 33435
(407) 738-6677

CLASSIC AUTO RACING SOCIETY (CARS)
1321 Beryl St., #306
Redondo Beach, CA 90277
(213) 374-5783

CHICAGO HISTORIC RACES (CHR)*
825 W. Erie St.
Chicago, IL 60622
(312) 829-7065

CORINTHIAN VINTAGE AUTO RACING (CVAR)
P.O. BOX 232
Addison, TX 75001
(214) 661-9030

HIGHLANDS CLASSIC
P.O. BOX 1652
Highlands, NC 28741

MEADOW BROOKS HISTORIC RACES (MBHR)
4140 S. Lapeer Rd.
Pontiac, MI 48057
(313) 373-2500

MOUNTAIN VIEW PROMOTIONS (MVP)*
P.O. BOX 3704
Littleton, CO 80161

NELSON LEDGES ROAD COURSE (NLRC)
3709 Valcamp Rd.
Warren, OH 44484

PITTSBURGH VINTAGE GP (PVGPA)*
P.O. BOX 2243
Pittsburgh, PA 15230
(412) 373-8440

PALM SPRINGS VINTAGE GP
330 E. Sunny Dunes Rd.
Palm Springs, CA 92264
(619) 320-9008

SCCA - VINTAGE
9033 E. Easter Pl.
Edgewood, CO
(303) 694-7222

VINTAGE AUTO RACING ASSOCIATION (VARA)*
3426 N. Knoll Dr.
Los Angeles, CA 90068
(213) 874-9135

WATERFORD HILLS ROAD RACING (WHRR)
4770 Waterford Rd.
Clarkston, MI 48016
(313) 493-3493

WALTER MITTY CHALLENGE (WMCVG)*
P.O. BOX 550372
Atlanta, GA 30355
(612) 471-0497

The Italian's (Alfa Romeo) and British (Triumph) do battle on the front straight at Road America (Wisconsin) during the 1989 VSCDA's Vintage Fall Festival.

Cliff Pass in his beautifully prepared 1967 Austin-Healey Sprite leads a bevy of small bore production models up the hill into turn 11 at Road Atlanta.

Westport Photoracing—Mike Farley

The Jag's of Bob O'Brien (#53) and Harry Warren (#49) at Moroso Park (Florida) during the SVRA's 1989 Spring Fling in March.

A pre-war 1934 Aston-Martin 'Ulster' at speed. These cars were the state of the art for high speed endurance racing and competed at Le Mans.

Cam-Am action with Walter Mitty's Steve Simpson ex Al Unser's Lola T332C through the esses at Road Atlanta.

Lotus enthusiast Bill Sandifer's lovely BMC powered Lotus VI at speed down the back stretch at Road Atlanta.

Heavy duty action in the big bore production class as a historic Mustang leads a Camaro and AMC Javelin at Mid-Ohio.

Bob Fergus's Lotus MK15 going head to head with a DB3 Aston-Martin at Moroso.

Porshe power at turn 5 during the 1989 Chicago Historic Races at Road America.

Vern Harvey's nicely prepared 1957 MGA roadster through the esses at Mid-Ohio.

The 904 GTS Porsche of Jeffery Keiner is followed closely by a Chevron B-19 in Can-Am action at Road Atlanta.

Terry McNeil's fast and competitive Mini-Cooper at Moroso.

CHAPTER VII

FIRST VINTAGE RACE...EXPECTATIONS and HELPFUL HINTS

"It is OK to finish last as long as you finish <u>safe</u> first"

The long awaited vintage race weekend has finally arrived. You have gone from a causal, interested spectator or crew member to an active participant in vintage racing. You have traded your binoculars and race program or perhaps tool chest and timing light for a Snell approved helmet and Nomex underwear. As any beginner, you are filled with anticipation, excitement and an understanding case of first round jitters, wondering how you and your vintage racer will perform during your first race event. To assist in overcoming your nervousness, and to inform other drivers of your rookie status, race organizers usually require first time drivers to show their "stripes" in the form of a symbol placed stategically on the rear of the car.

Remember, the main goals in vintage racing are having **fun** and **finishing**. Whether you are successful in accomplishing the above goals depends a great deal on the amount of preparation you have given yourself and car. The results could be very satisfying or a lasting disappointment depending on the time and energy spent on insuring you and your car are raceready. If you know your car has been properly and legally prepared, coupled with the knowledge of what it takes to drive fast at a safe speed, then the end results should be very positive, encouraging and a springboard to other exciting vintage racing adventures. Conversely, if you have not followed a prescribed routine of vintage car and driver preparation, and your philosophy on racing old cars is not in line with the spirit of vintage racing, then you might experience difficulty in successfully completing your first vintage race event.

What follows is a checklist to assist you in preventing and overcoming potential problems that would ruin an otherwise super race weekend. Be aware that this checklist should be used <u>prior</u> to arriving at the track. It is not all inclusive and can be changed depending on you and your car's particular situation and needs.

PRE-RACE CHECK LIST

BRAKES

OK	NEEDS ATTENTION	
——	——————	Pedal
——	——————	Lines/Connections
——	——————	Calipers/Drums
——	——————	Fluid
——	——————	Master Cylinder
——	——————	Pads/Shoes

Comments: _____
_____
_____

COOLING

OK	NEEDS ATTENTION	
——	——————	Radiator
——	——————	Fluid
——	——————	Water Pump
——	——————	Belts
——	——————	Hoses & Clamps
——	——————	Catch Tanks

Comments: _____
_____
_____

BODY

OK	NEEDS ATTENTION	
——	——————	Panels/Sheet Metal
——	——————	Mounts
——	——————	Finish & Trim
——	——————	Wash & Wax

Comments: _____
_____
_____

DRIVER

OK	NEEDS ATTENTION	
——	——————	Helmet
——	——————	Driving Suit
——	——————	Underwear
——	——————	Gloves/Shoes/Socks
——	——————	Accessories

Comments: _____
_____
_____

ENGINE

OK	NEEDS ATTENTION	
___	___	Oil
___	___	Filters
___	___	Ignition
___	___	Valve Adj.
___	___	Freeze Plugs
___	___	Carb
___	___	Fuel Lines
___	___	Leaks
___	___	Exhaust
___	___	Catch Tank

Comments: _____

_____

_____

DRIVETRAIN

OK	NEEDS ATTENTION	
___	___	Clutch (fluids)
___	___	Gearbox
___	___	U Joints
___	___	Differential
___	___	Drive Shaft
___	___	Catch Tank

Comments: _____

_____

SUSPENSION

OK	NEEDS ATTENTION	
___	___	General Inspect
___	___	Stub Axles
___	___	Wheel Bearings
___	___	Wheels & Spokes
___	___	Knock-Ons
___	___	Shocks & Springs

Comments: _____

_____

_____

STEERING

OK	NEEDS ATTENTION	
___	___	General Inspect (fluids)
___	___	Tie Rods
___	___	Arms & Wheel
___	___	Alignment
___	___	Ball Joints
___	___	Rack

Comments: _____

_____

_____

SAFETY

OK	NEEDS ATTENTION	
___	___	Gas Tank (fuel cell)
___	___	Gas Lines & Clamps
___	___	Mirrors
___	___	Tires (inflation)
___	___	Seat Belts
___	___	Roll Bar
___	___	Fire Extinguisher
___	___	Seat Mounts
___	___	Elec. Off Switch
___	___	Battery
___	___	Elec. Units & Connections

Comments: _____

_____

_____

OTHER

OK	NEEDS ATTENTION	
—	—	Tools
—	—	Jack & Stands
—	—	Portable Gas Container
—	—	Air Tank
—	—	Generator
—	—	Extra Fluids (oil, brake, ect.)
—	—	Accommodations
—	—	Log Book
—	—	Vintage License
—	—	Pit Crew
—	—	Spouse & Kids

Comments:_____
_____
_____

Comments:_____
_____
_____
_____
_____
_____
_____
_____
_____
_____
_____
_____
_____
_____
_____
_____
_____
_____
_____
_____
_____
_____

Besides preparing yourself and car, there are other things to consider which will help insure a successful weekend of racing. It is a good practice to arrive early at the track for the purpose of locating a place in the paddock that is convenient to other areas of the race track complex i.e. restrooms, concessions, gas pump facilities ect. Before the heat of competition, and prior to 'buckling up', it is always nice having easy access to Mother Nature. Preventing an accident in the paddock and false grid is just as important as preventing mishaps on the race track.

After registration and paddock space selection, you need to locate the tech inspection area. You can usually find this area where a long line of cars are backed up and waiting. Make it a habit to get your car inspected as soon as possible after arriving at the track. This practice allows you to use your valuable time in other ways than waiting in line for a tech inspection at the last minute.

Make sure you and your vintage racer are ready for Mr. Tech Inspector. In most cases, the Chief Tech Inspector (CTI) is a senior appointed member of the sponsoring vintage racing organization. He is basically a nice guy, who has been given the overwhelming task of 'teching' anywhere from 100 to 300+ cars. Usually, the CTI has 2-3 experienced assistants working for him. By all means, give them a break and understand their difficult plight and job. They are not out to get you and flag your car. The major reason there is a tech inspection is to insure that you and your car are safe for the task at hand. Also, insurance companies require that a tech inspection be done before you and your car are permitted on the track. The TI's are mainly interested in safety related items such as, roll bars, fire extinguishers, electrical cut-off switches, driving equipment etc. They will be looking as to whether these items are safely on board, properly installed and functioning. Also, if a tech inspector is knowledgeable about your car, he will probably check for improper modifications and changes in originality. During the tech inspection, have your log book ready and be prepared to answer questions about yourself and your vintage racer. You do not want to upset the person who has the power to prevent you from participating in the festivities. Total cooperation is the key to successfully passing tech inspection. Understand, the tech inspector is not the person responsible for the safety of your car. The ultimate responsibility rests on your shoulders, the driver/owner to insure all safety related items have met the standards set forth by the sponsoring racing organization. It is up to the CTI and his assistants to point out deficiencies and to disallow participation if safety standards fall below the norm.

Another good idea to help keep your head above water is to be aware at all times when your car is due on the false grid. Many veteran racers have a complete weekend race schedule handy in the paddock, placed in a location that cannot be missed or lost. Most vintage racing organizations like to see race groups grid up at least 10 minutes before scheduled track time. It is very disconcerting, disappointing and somewhat aggravating to watch your assigned race group tour the track from pit row as you realize you missed a practice session due to inattentiveness to the race program. Also, pay close attention to announced and scheduled driver meetings. These mandatory meetings are very helpful and productive in gathering information from the Chief Steward and his staff concerning flagging principles, safety and general track conditions. In addition, it is an excellent opportunity to socialize with other drivers and possibly find someone who would be willing to have a good 'dice' with you.

Obviously, practice sessions should be used to become familiar with the track. Do not be too aggressive your first time out - **TAKE IT SLOW AND WITH A PURPOSE**. If possible, get in the habit of walking the track before driving it. This important pre-race activity allows you the opportunity to get acquainted with the geometry of the turns, plus the fast and

slow areas of the track. During the 1989 VSCDA Vintage Fall Festival at Road America, a Porsche 911 Coupe, during its first practice session, took the first turn a little too aggressively - rolled twice, and ended up on its hardtop. Luckily, the 911 had a sturdy roll cage which prevented serious driver injury - but the Porsche sustained extensive damage and was eliminated from further participation. It is possible that if this driver would have taken the time to become familiar with the track, this accident might have been prevented.

Every turn on the race track has a correct entry and exit line. These lines depend on speed and the location of braking points. Use each practice session to determine the correct 'line' through the corner. Vary your speed and braking points until you feel comfortable and confident getting through the turn quickly and safely. An excellent method in determining the correct line is to follow someone experienced and knowledgeable about the track. Use the practice time to become familiar with your fellow competitors' driving habits and racing machinery. Know what cars are faster or slower compared to your car and other cars. Do not be intimidated by faster cars - use your mirrors, watch for the "passing flag" from the corner worker - move over, maintain your line and point to the side you want the faster car to pass. Both of you are responsible for a clean pass with the overtaking car having the greater responsibility. Pay strict attention to corner workers and the flags they display (see appendix). While on the track learning the correct line, practice using your mirrors. You will find that your mirrors are probably the most important safety items on your car. **USE THEM!!** Know what is happening behind and in front of you and be ready to act and react to sudden and unexpected events. Gathering all of the above information when practicing will definitely prove helpful when it is time for the featured race on Sunday.

On Sunday evening, after all the practice sessions, qualifying runs and the last checkered flag has fallen - while enjoying the camaraderie with family, friends, and fellow racers - you can look back on your first vintage race weekend with pride and a sense of accomplishment - knowing you **safely finished** as a **winner!!**

P.S. Don't forget to thank the race promoters and workers!

Art Eastman-Vintage Motorsport

JAMES WYANSKI ©'89

CHAPTER VIII

VINTAGE RACING...AN ENDURING PASTIME - THE FUTURE

"the future rests in the hands of enthusiasts who understand and practice the spirit of vintage racing"

Is the *racing* part of vintage racing a misnomer? Do we really "race" our vintage and historical automobiles? Yes and no - some people say we do - others disagree. One school of thought states that anytime you have one driver **wanting** to pass another driver i.e. **go faster,** a racing environment exists. Others say that 'racing', in the true sense of the word, does not exist in vintage racing. This leads us to another thought provoking question...What is considered **real** racing? I could probably exhaust a whole chapter discussing the many different opinions and answers to the above question.

In my mind *'real racing'* conjures up visions of <u>heated</u> wheel-to-wheel, thrash 'em and bang 'em up competition, where finishing first is paramount. This type of racing is found primarily in the professional ranks. If this was the prevalent attitude in vintage racing, the sport would not survive. Who in his (her) right mind would take a rare and expensive piece of classic racing machinery and "thrash" it around a race track all for the joy and glory of winning?? Vintage racing is not a venue for big egos who insist on being in the spotlight, where 'wanting to pass' and 'go faster' are the main goals. If you think this way, you need to find another activity to feed your ego and race your car. The SCCA folks have an excellent program for the 'racer' in us.

If the sport of vintage racing is to endure and prosper, all those involved need to cultivate and practice the *spirit* of vintage racing. We "vintage" race our cars not to win, go faster, or pass slower cars - but to show our special cars at speed, so all involved can share in the nostalgia and excitement of the past and present. From a driver and spectator viewpoint, there is nothing more exciting or alluring than to watch or be involved in a close <u>safe</u> dice (wheel-to-wheel) between 2 or 3 famous vintage racing automobiles. During the 1988 Chicago Historic Races, an exciting and memorable 'dice' took place between two famous Chevy-powered Scarab's from the past. Augie Pabst, driving a 1958 Scarab Mk2 and Don Orosco with his 1957 Scarab Mk1 thoroughly entertained and kept the crowd on its feet as they 'raced' around Road America's 4 mile roller coaster road course. The experience of watching those two beautifully sculptured, well-driven racing machines down-shifting into turn #5, fender-to-fender, V-8's bellowing is a memory that will linger in the minds of spectators for a long time.

Vintage racing is a vehicle which re-unites the Ford's, Vette's, Ferrari's and Scarab's of the past, while recreating automobile history in the present. At Sebring, Lime Rock and Road America famous marques of the past are competing once again as they did in the 50's, 60's and 70's. John Wyer's Ford GT-40's are again challenging the power and force of Jim Hall's GM V-8 driven Chapparal's at Sebring. The Vette's and the Cobra's of the 60's can again be seen at Road Atlanta and Mid-Ohio, recreating the famous and exciting rivalry that existed between these two racing giants of the past. A historic racing Jag or Porsche does not belong in a museum collecting dust and stares. They belong in their natural habitat - on a race track, at speed-where enthusiasts can see, smell, hear and enjoy them.

Art Eastman-Vintage Motorsport

In 1989, I had the opportunity to attend the Chicago Historic Races (CHR) at Elkhart Lakes's Road America. The CHR's is probably the premier vintage race event in the Midwest. Every year it brings out some of the best in vintage racing machinery from all over the country. I was amazed at the different array of interesting and valuable cars in the paddock. The amount of preparation and money involved just to participate was beyond my comprehension. There were close to 500 cars taking part in the weekend activities, which included touring, racing and a Concours de' Elegance. I estimated a total of 4-5 million($$$) invested in the total scene - which is a conservative figure and probably higher if I had the inclination to walk the paddock and ask on a individual basis what each participants'investment was in real money and on paper. In a way, based on the above observation, vintage racing is a phenomena that is somewhat hard to describe and understand. Why do we have people spending inordinate amounts of time, money and energy to prepare an 'old' and sometimes valuable piece of vintage machinery - and risk losing it all, just for the sake of participating in the sport we call VINTAGE RACING? Why does vintage racing exist? There are no financial rewards, front-page headlines, trophies, or even victory champagne waiting at the finish line. What is behind the popularity of vintage racing? What 'drives' the sport??

There are many reasons why people race old cars. One of the major reasons, and one that is very prominent, concerns the nostalgic factor (NF). All of us in some way or another would enjoy a return to our youth - to take another glimpse of ourselves from a different prospective. Some vintage racers are involved in the sport due to their participation in sports car racing in the 50's and 60's. They were racing today's "classics" a long time before some of us were breathing or walking. Although older in years, these 'veterans of the era' have an overabundance of racing experience which is obvious on the race track. They are the *true* racers of the modern vintage epoch. This class of racer has returned to the sport to re-create and re-live those wonderful experiences of actually *'being there'*—an exciting flashback to youthful innocence. Augie Pabst, a true veteran of the era and ardent vintage racing enthusiasts says, "vintage racing reminds me of the SCCA in the 50's and early 60's where we raced for fun and weekends were relaxed with friends helping each other." Other enthusiasts have taken a cue from James Thurber's famous character, Walter Mitty, who dreamed of becoming "that suave devil-may-care-race car driver" that we would all like to be. In every vintage racing enthusiast a little of 'Walter Mitty' exists - where our dreams do become real. Another reason, and one that affects my involvement in vintage racing is the love I have for classic automobiles. Vintage racing is an excellent way to experience those classic and historical automobiles you have heard or read about but never see. I find vintage racing exciting for the simple reason that it gives me the unique opportunity of experiencing first-hand famous and historic automobiles of the past. Reading about these cars can be interesting, but to share the same track and paddock is quite a different story. To be able to rub elbows with some of the famous race drivers of the past allows an enthusiast, like myself, to look at automobile racing history from a different prospective.

I remember my pulse quickening and euphoria erupting when a rare, historical '57' Aston-Martin DBR2, driven by Stirling Moss, blew by me and my relatively stock Austin-Healey 3000 during the 1986 Grand Bahama Vintage Grand

Prix (GBVGP). The scene comes back to me almost in slow motion as the big-bore DBR2 approaches in my rear-view mirrors - me pointing the way for His imminent pass- and Him waving a polite thank you as He safely overtakes me. Seeing the same DBR2 in a car museum with a placard telling me that Mr. Moss once drove this car to victory at Nurburgring would be interesting, but hardly exciting compared to my exhilarating experience at the GBVGP.

Vintage racing brings out the <u>best</u> in us - and in some cases, if we are not careful - it also brings out the worst. Presently, there are some people involved in vintage racing who should take a close look at themselves and determine whether their philosophy and reasons for participating are in line with the vintage racing spirit. If you are out of sync, then you need to look elsewhere for excitement, before you ruin the sport for the true enthusiast. Unfortunately, due to overdriving and a lack of concern of some vintage drivers, many rare and famous racing cars of the past are disappearing from race events. Their owners are withdrawing because they feel in some ways vintage racing has become too competitive and they do not want to risk destroying a part of auto racing history. Everyone loses

Westport Photoracing—Mike Farley

when a rare, historical racing machine, formerly active in vintage racing, becomes once again a museum piece only for discussion and wonderment.

Read carefully the following editorial which first appeared in the second issue of the popular vintage racing monthly magazine - <u>VICTORY LANE</u> back in 1986. It does a nice job defining vintage racing.

EDITORIAL
VICTORY LANE MAGAZINE May, 1986

THE SPORT OF VINTAGE RACING

Some forms of auto racing are for sport and some are professional. Vintage and historic racing is a sport. Sports are considered to be games, and all games have rules to keep the game fair, and to insure that the sport remains safe for participants.

Everyone needs to abide by the rules or the game is no longer fun and the rules have to be enforced so that everyone plays fair. No one in vintage racing should have anything to prove; that is not the point of the sport. Racing is not the key word here - fun and participation are.

Many of you would not be involved in this sport if there was the very serious chance that every time you took to the track you and/or your automobile were going to get banged up. Believe me, we would be just as happy to listen to your sad tale of finishing last, as we would of your heroics of finishing first.

This is a sport recreating 'Gentleman Racing', where you are expected to conduct yourself as such. The fact that you have brought a vintage racer back from the past to share with all of us should be satisfaction enough. Vintage racing is a growing sport in the United States, but major accidents and injuries can stop it in its tracks.

I remind you, ladies and gentlemen, play by the rules, be safe, enjoy yourself and have fun. And I strongly encourage all race groups and promoters - enforce your rules! Bad apples spoil the barrel, and unless you pluck them out, the barrel will rot.

The sport of vintage racing is a game of fun. **BE A WINNER!!**

Dewey Dellinger
Editor
VICTORY LANE MAGAZINE

The future of vintage racing-the **staying power**, rests in the hands of enthusiasts who understand the intrinsic worth and value of preserving, restoring and racing vintage automobiles. All involved, especially the participants and vintage racing organizations, need to safeguard the spirit of the sport by following and enforcing certain principles that will allow vintage racing to remain a positive pastime experience worth pursuing and practicing. Do not lose the vision i.e. the *spirit* of why vintage racing exists - **TO SHOW OUR VINTAGE AND HISTORICAL AUTOMOBILES AT SPEED - FOR ALL TO SHARE IN THE EXPERIENCE AND ENJOYMENT OF THEIR HISTORY, FUNCTION AND BEAUTY.**

John DeMaria's very fast and competitive Lotus 11 Climax S1 'at speed' during the 1989 Vintage Grand Prix AuGrattan in Michigan.

CHAPTER IX

LASTING IMPRESSIONS...COOL DOWN LAP

VINTAGE MOTORSPORTS COUNCIL (VMC)

In 1988, some of the vintage racing organizations due to the wide growth of the sport and diversification of locality between the different organizations, founded the VINTAGE MOTORSPORTS COUNCIL. This group is composed of members from each racing organization, who meet on a regular basis to formulate and discuss vintage racing policy. They also act as a forum for the purpose of sharing and solving common problems that relate to vintage racing in general. An important VMC responsibility is to compile and maintain a list of drivers who violate the "13/13 Rule" and report this list to other VMC member vintage racing organizations on a monthly basis. The VMC has established lines of communication between the major organizers of vintage races, general guidelines for car and driver safety and eased scheduling conflicts. The 18 member VMC has also undertaken to issue a national vintage racing license - to facilitate drivers moving across club lines. At the moment, the VMC seems to be the easiest answer to the need for a National authority which will allow local clubs to retain the rules which each has dictated.

"7/10 vs. 10/10"

A popular phrase used amongst vintage race drivers that describes the relative speed i.e., effort that drivers should practice (7/10) as opposed to the all out effort that is seen in professional racing (10/10).

HELMET MEDICAL INFORMATION

A good common sense practice is to place on the back of your race helmet a sticker that states your name, bloodtype, allergies and person(s) to notify in case of an emergency:

NAME:
BLOOD-TYPE:
ALLERGIES:
EMERGENCY:

Many of the vintage racing organizations require the above information on helmets.

LOG BOOKS

Most VRO's require a record of vintage racing events and tech inspections for you and your car. Every time you enter an event, present your Log Book to the tech inspectors for review and comment. An accurate, up-to-date Log Book will help you get through tech inspection quickly. After use, put it in a safe place - it is your key to a hassle free tech inspection. In addition, to assisting in tech inspection, a Log Book is an important document that shows the past history of a car in relation to competition and safety. **DON'T LEAVE HOME WITHOUT IT!**

INSURANCE

Depending on your investment in vintage racing, you might want to purchase some on-track insurance for yourself and car. There are specialty insurance companies who cater to the needs of race car drivers (see Business Directory). As part of your race entry, the major VRO's provide on-track liability, but many times not nearly enough to cover a major catastrophe. Incidentally, a part of your entry fee goes for insurance that covers you just in case you happen to hit a spectator or damage the track. If I had a rare, million $$$ vintage racing Ferrari (wishful thinking), there is little doubt I would be paying a hefty insurance premium to protect my valuable investment.

CORNER WORKERS

Some of the nicest people in vintage racing are the corner workers. These folks play an important role in safety, insuring we all go home with pleasant smiles after a grueling race weekend. They are dedicated volunteer workers who, like ourselves, enjoy being around old race cars. Usually, if there is trouble on the track, the corner workers are the first on the scene helping to rectify the problem, The next time you take your cool-down lap, after finishing an exciting race, make sure you take the time to show them a little appreciation in form of a "thumbs up" gesture. It gives them a good feeling knowing they did their job watching out for your safety and well-being. After reading this book you decide that the driving part of vintage racing is not for you, for whatever reasons, consider joining one of the corner worker organizations or a 'behind the scene' position and still continue your involvement in the sport.

RACE TRACKS

The following is a list of major tracks with sponsoring vintage racing organizations that host vintage race events:

TRACKS	STATE/COUNTRY	VRO
1. Au Grattan	MI	VSCDA
2. Laguna Seca	CA	HMSA/VMR
3. Lime Rock	CT	VSCCA
4. Firebird	AZ	ARSA
5. Mid-Ohio	OH	SVRA
6. Moroso	FL	CARE/SVRA
7. Mountain View	CO	RMVR
8. Mosport	Canada	VARAC
9. Portland	WA	SOVREN
10. Road America	WI	VSCDA
11. Road Atlanta	GA	SVRA
12. Sears Point	CA	VMC/CSRG
13. Sebring	FL	SVRA
14. Watkins Glen	NY	SVRA
15. Willow Springs	CA	VARA

TRACK NOTES

ROAD ATLANTA
Rt 1
Braselton, GA 30517
(404) 967-6143

— 2.5 mile road course located in the red clay Georgia hills 40 miles NE of Atlanta.

— plays host to IMSA, CART and SCCA events; annual SCCA Championship in October (Fall Run-Offs).

— excellent track for spectating and driving; modern facilities; 12 turns; .5 mile front-straightaway; for spectating try the

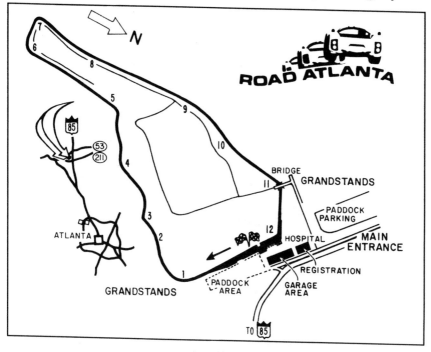

Esses and Turn #11 (blind curve-downhill); SVRA & WMC vintage events.

SEBRING INTERNATIONAL RACEWAY
— located middle of Florida; east of Palm Beach, west of Fort Meyers; steeped in motor racing history.

— new 4.1 mile circuit with 13 turns; 12 Hours of Sebring (IMSA); SVRA sponsored vintage event; plenty of excellent spectator views & areas.

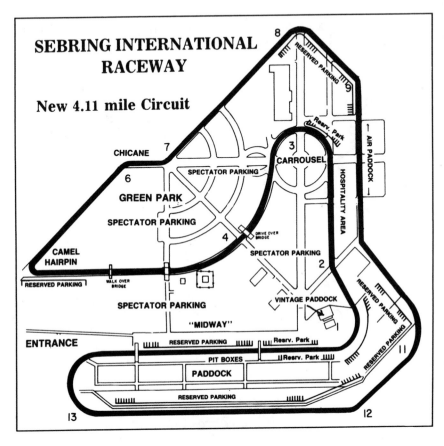

SEBRING INTERNATIONAL RACEWAY

New 4.11 mile Circuit

LAGUNA SECA RACEWAY
— located due east of Monterey, California on land once occupied by the Army's Fort Ord.

— 2.1 (new) mile circuit with 11 turns; host Monterey Historic Races, IMSA and CART events; famous corkscrew turn (#8); excellent modern facilities with super spectating views.

MID-OHIO
— located between Columbus and Mansfield, Ohio; 2.4 mile road course with 15 turns.

— plays host to SVRA vintage event in June, plus several professional and SCCA events throughout the year; beautiful modern facilities; long back stretch; best spectator views are the Esses between turns 6 & 8 and Carrousel between turns 13 & 15 leading into the front straight.

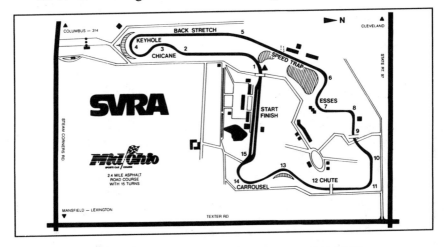

SEARS POINT INTERNATIONAL RACEWAY
— nestled in the rolling hills of the Sonoma, California wine country; 45 minutes north of San Francisco.

— 2.5 mile, 12 turn road racing circuit with 150′ elevation changes; exceptional spectator viewing areas; camping permitted; plays host to CSRG and VMR vintage racing events.

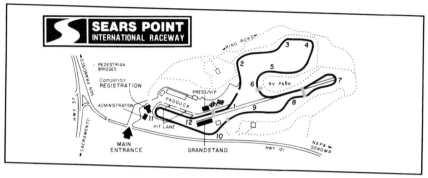

WILLOW SPRINGS INTERNATIONAL RACEWAY
Box X
Rosamond, CA 93560
(805) 256-2471

— known as the fastest 2.5 mile 9 turn road course in the West; 2400' front straight; camping permitted; off road testing and rally areas; VARA racing events.

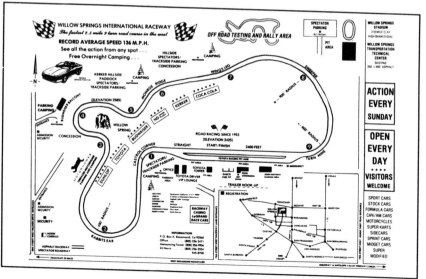

ROAD AMERICA Elkhart Lake, WI 53020

— located 60 miles north of Milwaukee near Elkhart Lake (resort area).

— 4 mile 14 turn road course with plenty of challenging turns; beautiful spectating areas i.e. turn #5 before Nissan bridge; course record 122.5 MPH - 1:57.5 set by Mark Donahue (Porsche-Audi) 1973; host VSCDA and CHR events.

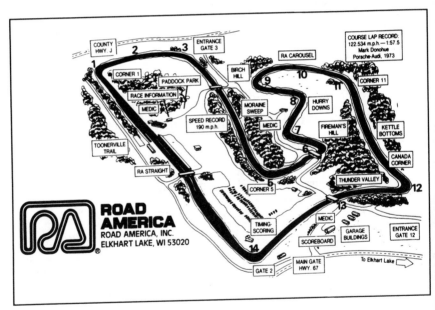

MOUNTAIN VIEW   4113 Weld County Rd
P.O. Box 687
Mead Co., CO 80542
(303) 535-4907

— located 30 miles north of Denver and 70 miles south of Cheyenne, Wyoming.

— 1.8 mile road track with 10 turns; elevation 5000'; plays host to RMVR events.

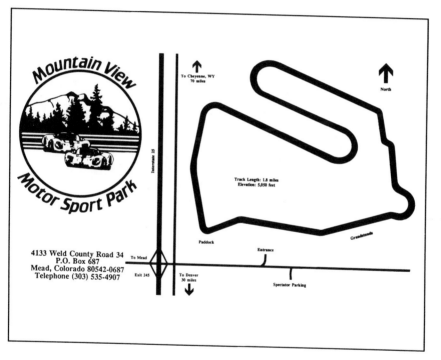

A Cam-Am Porsche through turns 5 & 6 at Road Atlanta with a North American Racing Team (NART) Ferrari in hot pursuit.

APPENDIX A

ROLL BAR SPECIFICATIONS

VEHICLE WEIGHT:	TUBING SIZE:
less than 1500 lbs.	1.50" dia x .120 wall thickness
1500 lbs. to 2500 lbs.	1.75 dia x .120 wall thickness
over 2500 lbs.	2.25 dia x .120 wall thickness

1. The dimensions given above are for mild steel tubing. Specifications for alloy tubing can be found in the SCCA's "General Competition Rules" book.

2. Fore/aft bracing must be at an angle of 30 degrees or more from the main hoop (measured from vertical).

3. One continuous length of tubing should be used for the main hoop member with smooth continous bends and no evidence of crimping or wall failure.

4. The main hoop attaching points should not be less than 15 inches apart.

5. All bolts used in roll bar installation must be at least 3/8 " diameter and of SAE Grade 5 or better.

6. All mounting plates must be at least 3/16 inch thick and of sufficient size to spread the load. Bolt-on bars must have back-up plates of the same dimensions as the mounting plates or better.

REQUIRED SHOULDER HARNESS MOUNTING

1.   The shoulder harness must be mounted behind the driver and at no more that a 40 degree angle for the horizontal (measured from the driver's shoulder); the minumum acceptable bolts used in the mounting of all belts or harness is SAE Grade 5. (see diagram)

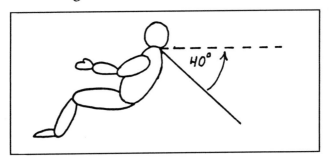

(The above information courtesy of RMVR)

RULES OF THE ROAD (FLAGGING PROCEDURES)

1.   FLAGS

-GREEN—The race is underway at the instant the flag falls and from then on means the course is clear.

-YELLOW—When motionless: take care, danger, **NO PASS-ING** until past emergency area. When yellow is waved: great danger, be prepared to **STOP; NO PASSING** until past emergency area.

-RED—Stop **IMMEDIATELY**; clear the circuit as well as circumstances allow; the race has been stopped.

-BLUE with DIAGONAL YELLOW STRIPE—When motionless another competitor is following closely; when waved a faster competitor is trying to overtake (pass); **CHECK YOUR MIRRORS**.

-YELLOW with VERTICAL RED STRIPES—Take care, oil has been spilled and/or slippery conditions exist on the circuit; debris present on the track.

-WHITE—An ambulance or service vehicle is on the course; or slow moving vehicle on the course.

-BLACK—Complete the lap you are on then **STOP** for consultation at the location designated by the Chief Steward as the black flag station.

-BLACK with ORANGE BALL—There is something mechanically wrong with your car; reduce speed and proceed to the pit area.

-CHECKERED—You have finished the race (or practice session); complete one more lap (cool down) cautiously before returning to the pit area.

2. PASSING

Passing may be limited to areas specified by the Chief Steward. The responsibility for the decision to pass another car rests with the overtaking driver, and must be done safely. However, this will not relieve the overtaken driver of the responsibility for the safe passing of the other car. An overtaken driver should point to the side on which the overtaking driver should pass. Any driver who fails to use his mirrors, or appears to be blocking another car, may be black flagged.

3. HAND SIGNALS

In addition to the above, a driver should signal his entry into the pit area by raising one arm. The driver of a stalled car should raise both arms to indicate that he will not move until the course is clear.

4. RE-ENTRY

In the event a driver leaves the course, re-entry may only occur with the permission of a flagperson (corner worker) and must be done in a safe manner.

5. STOPPING

Stopping on the course in emergencies should be done so as not to cause danger or obstruction to other vehicles.

Race Flags

GREEN The Race has started, the course is clear.

YELLOW (Motionless) Take care. Danger. No passing. (Waved) Great danger. Be prepared to stop. No passing.

RED STOP IMMEDIATELY. Clear the circuit as well as circumstances permit.

BLACK Stop at your pit IMMEDIATELY. Do not pass Start-Finish line.

BLUE (Motionless) Another competitor is trying to pass. (Waved) MOVE OVER, let faster vehicle pass.

WHITE An ambulance or service car is on the circuit.

YELLOW, RED STRIPES Take care. Debris has been spilled somewhere on the track.

CHECKERED You have finished the race, complete one more lap at reduced speed before stopping.

ADDITIONAL READING

1. Engine Blueprinting: A Step-by-Step Guide, by Rick Voegelin 1985.
2. Performance Tuning in Theory & Practice: Four Strokes, by Graham Bell 1981.
3. The Sports Car: Its Design and Performance, by Colin Campbell 1978.
4. Handling and Roadholding: Car Suspension at Work, by Jeffrey Daniels.
5. The BMC/BL Competitions Department: 25 Years in Motor Sport - the Cars, the People, the Events, by Bill Price.
6. The History of Motor Racing, by William Broody & Brian Laban.
7. Directory of Historic Racing Cars, by Denis Jenkinson.
8. The Restoration and Preservation of Vintage & Classic Cars, by Jonathan Wood 1984.
9. The Art of Motor Racing, by Emerson Fittipaldi & Gordon Kirby.
10. Bob Bondurant on High Performance Driving, by Bob Bondurant.
11. The Cars of BMC, by Graham Robson.
12. BMC & Leyland B Series Engine Data, by Lindsey Porter.
13. Tuning BL's A-Series Engine, by David Vizard.
14. Vintage & Historic Racing Cars, by Alex Gabbard 1986.
15. Directory of Classic Sports-Racing Cars, by Mike Lawrence 1987.
16. Adventure on Wheels, by John Fitch 1959.

APPENDIX B

VINTAGE RACING BUSINESS DIRECTORY
(VRBD)

The below listed vintage racing businesses helped support the production of this book. Please support them when purchasing vintage racing related parts, supplies and services.

RACING SUPPLIES & EQUIPMENT

STAND 21 U.S.A.
2872 Walnut Ave
Tustin, CA 92680
(714) 838-7031
FAX (714) 731-8651
Driver Suits & Equipment

HALO PRODUCTS
1538 MacArthur Blvd
Oakland, CA 94602
800-366-4256
in CA (415) 531-2211
Discount Bell Helmets, Driving Suits & Equipment

GEMINI RACING SYSTEMS INC
7802 E Gray Rd #300
Scottsdale, AZ 85260
(602) 948-8101
(602) 991-9831
Racing Software, Computers, Books, Driver Equipment

PEGASUS AUTO RACING SUPPLIES INC
2475 S 179th St
New Berlin, WI 53146
(414) 782-0880
FAX 414-782-0484
General Racing Hardware, Tools, Equipment & Supplies

WREP IND INC
1529 Burgundy Pkwy
Streamwood, IL 60107
(708) 213-1515
Driver & Safety Equipment
and Supplies

**RAPID MOTIONS,
LIMITED**
P.O. Box 1006
Danville, CA 94526
(415) 736-8462
Fax 415-525-8658
Wide range of driving equipment and supplies

RACE PARTS

HALIBRAND ENGINE INC
9344 Wheatlands Rd
Santee, CA 92072
562-7930
General Race Parts, Hewland
Parts & Rear Ends ect.

VICTORIA BRITISH LTD
14600 W 107 St, Box 14991
Lenexa, KS 66215
800-255-0088
FAX 913-599-FAXX
(913) 541-8500
British Car Parts & Supplies

ED SWART MOTORS INS.
2675 Sky Park Drive
Torrance, CA 90505
(213) 530-9715
Distributor of parts for vintage Chevron Race Cars

THE PARTS SHOP
15725 Chemical Ln
Huntington Beach, CA 92649
(714) 894-3112
Bill Perrone - Owner
Porsche Parts & Vintage Race
Prep

SCARTI
859 N Hollywood Way, #409
Burbank, CA 91505
Distributor for Ginetta Cars &
Parts

JOE CURTO INC
230-22 58th Ave
Bayside, NY 11364
(718) 465-4829
SU Carbs Parts & Overhaul;
Pre-war to Post

BRITISH RACER USA
R3 Box 45
Sparta, WI 54656
(608) 269-5591
(608) 388-3110
High Performance British
Parts for Road & Track

ALFA RICAMBI
6644 San Fernando Rd
Glendale, CA 91201
(818) 956-7433
Alfa Parts

DRE INC
1529 Burgundy Pkwy
Streamwood, IL 60107
(708) 213-1010
Formula Vee Parts & Services

WINNER'S CIRCLE
19144 Detroit Rd
Rocky River, OH 44116
(216) 333-4666
British Race Parts & Supplies

**PERFORMANCE
ENGINEERING LTD**
2375 N Fifth
Springfield, OR 97477
(503) 746-9714
Custom British Race parts

MOSS MOTORS LTD
7200 Hollister Ave
P.O. Box MG
Goleta, CA 93116
(805) 968-1041
FAX 805-968-6910
TELEX 65473
World's Largest Supplier of
British Parts

INSURANCE

**COOPER, LOVE &
JACKSON**
1804 Hayes St
Nashville, TN 37203
800-274-1804
On/Off Track Insurance (including transportation)

**HEACOCK INSURANCE
AGENCY**
Lakeland, FL
813-646-6641
High limits protection for
Historic Racing Cars

PUBLICATIONS

**VICTORY LANE
MAGAZINE**
2460 Park Blvd, Suite #4
Palo Alto, CA 94306
(415) 321-4426

**GRASSROOTS
MOTORSPORTS**
P.O. Drawer A
Daytona Beach, FL 32188
800-423-1780

VINTAGE MOTORSPORT
P.O. Box 2895
Lakeland, FL 33806
(813) 686-3104

BRITISH CAR
P.O. Box 9099
Canoga Park, CA 91309
(818) 710-1234

VINTAGE PREP

ENTROPY RACING
865 Airport Rd
Monterey, CA 93940
(408) 375-5975
Cobra & Alfa Romeo Prep and
Maintenance

**TRACO ENGINEERING
INC**
11928 W Jefferson Blvd
Culver City, CA 90230
(213) 398-3722
Vintage Race Engine Prep

**HANS ROCKE
ENTERPRISES**
P.O. Box 1871, Rt 44
Lakeville, CT 06039
(203) 435-0177
Vintage Prep & Enclosed
Transport

KTR ENGINEERING INC
Box 560
Groton, MA 01450
(508) 772-7800
Prep, Service, Restoration

THE ENGINE ROOM
318 A, River St
Santa Cruz, CA 95060
(408) 429-1800
Race Prep & Parts for
Triumph, MG, Alfa, & Others

AUTO MARINE ENGINES
1005 Huntley Road
Algonquin, IL 60102
(708) 658-2233
Complete Machine Shop and
Parts

THE MACHINE WORKS
42736 Mound Road
Sterling Heights, MI 48310
(313) 739-0808
Machine & Fabrication of race
car parts

**MANARELLO IMPORT
AUTO SERVICE**
748 San Antonio Road
Palo Alto, CA 94303
(415) 494-1785
British & Italian Mechanicals

PROFESSIONAL DRIVING SCHOOLS

ROAD ATLANTA
Rt 1, Hwy 53
Braselton, GA 30517
(404) 967-6143

VINTAGE RESTORATION

**INTREPID
MOTORCAR CO**
1665 Linda Way
Sparks, NV 89431
(702) 356-7389
Restoration, Service & Maintenance

**NORMAN RACING
GROUP**
1221 Fourth St
Berkeley, CA 94710
(415) 525-1164
Component Repair & Fabrication

THE BUCKINGHAM SERVICE
10944 Grissom, Suite 701-704
Dallas, TX 75229
(214) 247-2654
Restoration of British Motorcars

LeGRAND RACE CARS
HCR 3, Box 181
Willow Springs Raceway
Rosamond, CA 93560
(805) 256-3837
Vintage Restorations, Koni Shocks, Coil-Over Springs

TOM RUST RACING
28019 Arnold Dr
Sears Point Raceway
Sonoma, CA 95476
(707) 938-4020
Restoration, Race Prep, Engine Rebuilding

AUTO RESTORATIONS INC (Vintage Racing Div)
1785 Barnum Ave
Stratford, CT 06497
(203) 377-6745
Restoration, Prep, Lotus/British Specialist

CHRIS SMITHS' CREATIVE WORKSHOP
118 NW Park St
Dania, FL 33004
(305) 920-3303
Restoration, Parts, Tuning, Fabrication ect.

TRANSPORTATION

PASSPORT TRANSPORT LTD
37 Progress Pkwy
St. Louis, MO 63043
800-325-4267
Auto Transport

VINTAGE SALES & SERVICES

SPYDER MOTORSPORTS
P.O. Box 712
Orlando, FL 32802
(407) 843-2111
Investment & Sales; Full-line of Services

AM RACING INC
P.O. Box 451
Danvers, MA 01923
(508) 774-4613
Sales Vintage & Historic Race Cars

INTERNATIONAL AUTO GROUP OF NORTH AMERICA INC
San Juan, Puerto Rico; Clarksville, TN; Tomah, WI
(608) 372-6958
Sales & Service; Manufacture of Porsche-Spyder Replica with genuine Porsche Components

NEW ENGLAND CLASSIC
1785 Barnum Ave.
Stratford, CT 06497
(203) 377-6746
Sales, Service, Resto

WHEELS & TIRES

DAYTON WHEEL PRODUCTS
1147 S Broadway
Dayton, OH 45408
(513) 461-1707
Restoration & Sales of Wire Wheels

NORTHUMBERLAND ENGINEERING CORP
118 Mariner Dr
Southampton, NY 11968
(516) 287-2213
Importer & Distributor Dunlop Vintage Racing Tires

RODGER KRAUS RACING
INC
2896 Grove Way
Castro Valley, CA 94546
(415) 582-5031
Avon Tires; Goodyear Race &
Street; Dunlop Vintage

OTHER

VINTAGE SPORTS CAR
PROMOTIONS
345 California Ave, Suite 4
Palo Alto, CA 94306
(415) 321-3336

JAMES WYANSKI JR.
511 Division Street
Scotia, NY 12302
(518) 372-4360
Artist for Classic & Historical
Automobiles

MOTORSPORT
INTERNATIONAL
PUBLISHING CO. (MIPCO)
R3 Box 45
Sparta, WI 54656
(608) 269-5591
Publisher of Automobile Racing Books and Journals

WESTPORT
PHOTORACING
c/o Mike Farley
P.O. Box 413222
Kansas City, MO 64141
(816) 444-6589
Vintage race car photography

INDEX

ABOUT THE AUTHOR

The author, Jim McCarthy, a dentist by profession, has been an active participant in vintage racing since 1983. His first 'racing experience' occurred at Road Atlanta while campaigning a 1960 Austin-Healey 3000 during a SVRA event. He is a member of SVRA, VSCDA and VSCR and holds a competition Vintage Motorsport Council (VMC) license.

In addition to his vintage racing experiences, Dr. McCarthy has written numerous articles for auto clubs and associations. He has also written and photographed racing events for the monthly vintage racing magazine VICTORY LANE. When not pursuing journalistic endeavors, Dr. McCarthy's preferred vintage racing machinery is a 1960 MGA Coupe.

Another book on vintage racing entitled, *VINTAGE PRO-FILES*, is currently being researched and written for publication towards the end of 1990.

FOR ADDITIONAL COPIES OF *VINTAGE RACING!! START TO FINISH* PLEASE CONTACT THE FOLLOWING ADDRESS, or COMPLETE ENCLOSED ORDER FORM.
Ms. Alicia Uhlman (MIPCO)
4703 Parklane Drive
Kearney, NE 68847

The author, Jim McCarthy and his vintage race prepared 1960 MGA Coupe.

DID YOU BORROW THIS BOOK?
WANT A COPY OF YOUR OWN?
NEED A GREAT GIFT FOR A FRIEND OR FELLOW ENTHUSIAST?

ORDER FORM

Yes, I want a personal copy of this book. Send_____ copy(ies) of *Vintage Racing!! Start to Finish* at $19.95 per book.

Please add $2.00 per book for postage and handling. Wisconsin residents include 5% state sales tax. (Canadian orders must be accompanied by a postal money order in U.S. funds.) Allow 30 days for delivery. Send check/money order payable to:

RPM Enterprises Ltd. (MIPCO)
Rt. 3 Box 45
Sparta, WI 54656.

Name _____ Phone

Address _____

City _____ State _____ Zip _____

Here's my check/money order for $_____

QUANTITY ORDERS INVITED

For bulk discount prices please call (608) 269-5591

NOTES

NOTES